11/07

The Rosen Comprehensive
Dictionary of
Physics

Edited by
John O.E. Clark and William Hemsley

ROSEN
PUBLISHING®

New York

Published by The Rosen Publishing Group, Inc.
29 East 21st Street, New York, N.Y. 10010

Rosen Comprehensive edition © 2008 by The Rosen Publishing Group, Inc.

First Edition

Library of Congress Cataloging-in-Publication Data

The Rosen comprehensive dictionary of physics.
    p. cm.
 ISBN-13: 978-1-4042-0702-8
 ISBN-10: 1-4042-0702-3 (library binding)
 1. Physics--Dictionaries. I. Rosen Publishing Group. II. Title: Dictionary of physics.
 QC5R595 2007
 530.03--dc22
                          2006032645

Manufactured in the United States of America

Preface

The Rosen Comprehensive Dictionary of Physics has been devised
for two main groups of readers. The first group consists of people
whose daily work brings them into contact with terms from
physics. They may be industrial physicists or—because of the
nature of their jobs—non-physicists who nevertheless have to
understand specialist terminology. Readers in the second category
are students, and for them we have tried to meet several needs.
Students who are learning physics will find the dictionary
invaluable for checking the meanings of words that are a required
part of the vocabulary of the subject. Students in allied disciplines,
such as biology, chemistry, engineering and medicine, can use it
as a handy reference source for words from physics that are
commonly employed in *their* subjects, but are so often taken for
granted.

The overlap of physics with other disciplines posed a problem
for the compilers of this dictionary. There is an inevitable link
between physics and the other sciences, particularly because in one
sense physics is fundamental to all science. So where does physics
stop and another science, such as chemistry, begin? Obviously, the
main terms of theoretical physics have to be included in the
dictionary, as does some of the terminology of more practical sides
of the subject, which relates physics to topics such as engineering.
However, there comes a point where the realm of physics must be
regarded as coming to an end. For example, physics deals with
the structure and particles of the atoms, but—with minor
exceptions—bonding interactions between atoms and the study
of molecules are certainly a part of chemistry and belong better to
The Rosen Comprehensive Dictionary of Chemistry, which is a
companion volume to this one. Similarly, while vector quantities
are an essential part of physics, the study of complex statics and
dynamics may be regarded as being in the realm of the engineer
and the applied mathematician.

A

aberration Production of an optical image with colored fringes that occurs because the focal length of a lens is different for different colors of light (chromatic aberration) so that the lens focuses different colors in different planes; or the production of an image that is not sharp when a beam of light falls on the edges as well as on the center of a lens (spherical aberration).

absolute humidity Amount of water vapor in a given volume of air, also called vapor concentration. *See also* **relative humidity**.

absolute temperature Fundamental temperature scale used in theoretical physics and chemistry. It is expressed in kelvin (K), corresponding to the **Celsius scale**. Zero is taken as **absolute zero**. Alternative name: thermodynamic temperature.

absolute unit Unit defined in terms of units of fundamental quantities such as length, time, mass and electric charge or current.

absolute zero Lowest temperature theoretically possible, at which a substance has no heat energy whatsoever. It corresponds to –273.15°C, or 0 K on the kelvin scale.

absorptance α Ability of a medium to absorb radiation. It is the ratio of the total radiation absorbed by a medium to the total radiation arriving at its surface. Alternative name: absorptivity.

absorption Taking up of matter or energy by other matter; *e.g.,* cold metal placed in hot water absorbs heat energy and illuminated objects absorb some of the light that falls on them.

absorption spectrum Characteristic pattern of dark lines that is seen in a **spectrum** produced when light is passed through a selectively absorbing medium.

absorptivity Alternative name for **absorptance**.

a.c. Abbreviation of **alternating current**.

acceleration (a) Rate of change of velocity; its SI units are ms^{-2} (meters per second per second). If velocity changes at a constant rate from an initial value of u to a final value of v in a time t, acceleration a is given by $a = (v - u) / t$. Alternatively if velocity is represented by v, acceleration is found by differentiating v with respect to time t; *i.e.*, acceleration $a = dv/ dt$. *See also* **force**.

acceleration due to gravity *See* **acceleration of free fall**.

acceleration of free fall (g) **Acceleration** given to an object by the gravitational attraction of Earth. It has an international standard value of 9.80665 ms^{-2}. Alternative name: acceleration due to gravity.

accelerator 1. Machine that increases the **kinetic energy** of an object or particle, *e.g.*, a **particle accelerator**. 2. Mechanism that controls the speed of an electric motor or engine (by controlling the amount of current of fuel supplied). Alternative name: throttle.

access time Period of time required for reading out of, or writing into, a computer's memory.

achromatic lens Combination of two or more lenses that has a **focal length** that is the same for two or more different **wavelengths** of light. This arrangement largely overcomes chromatic **aberration**.

acoustics 1. Science of the production, containment and movement of sound. 2. Qualities of a building with regard to the behavior of sound within it.

acoustoelectronics Branch of **electronics** concerned with the use of sound waves at **microwave** frequencies.

actinic radiation Electromagnetic radiation (particularly ultraviolet radiation) that can cause a chemical reaction.

action Alternative name for **force**.

activated carbon Charcoal treated so as to be a particularly good absorbent of gases.

adder Part of a computer that adds digital signals (addend, augend and a carry digit) to produce the sum and a carry digit.

address In computing, 1. identity of a location's position in a memory or store, or 2. specification of an operand's location.

adhesion Attraction between different substances (at the atomic or molecular level); *e.g.,* between water particles and glass, creating a **meniscus**. See also **cohesion**.

adiabatic process Process that occurs without interchange of heat with the surroundings.

admittance *(Y)* Property that allows the flow of electric current across a **potential difference**; the reciprocal of **impedance**.

adsorbent Substance on which **adsorption** takes place.

adsorption Accumulation of **molecules** or **atoms** of an advanced substance (usually a gas) on the surface of another substance (a solid or a liquid).

advanced gas-cooled reactor (AGR) Type of nuclear **reactor** that uses carbon dioxide as a coolant.

advection Transfer of heat or matter (*e.g.,* water vapor) associated with the horizontal movement of an air mass through the atmosphere.

aerial Wire, rod or other device that is used to transmit or receive radio waves. The simplest aerials are lengths of wire or ferrite rods employed in domestic radio receivers. Transmitting aerials are often large structures, sometimes more than 328 ft tall. Microwave aerials usually take the form of a dish. Alternative name: antenna.

aerodynamics Study of the motion of solid objects in air, or of moving gases.

aerogenerator Electrical **generator** that is driven by wind power.

aerosol 1. Suspension of particles of a liquid or solid in a gas; a type of **colloid**. 2. Device used to produce such a suspension.

agonic line Line drawn on a map that connects places at which the **magnetic declination** is zero.

AGR Abbreviation of **advanced gas-cooled reactor**.

air Mixture of gases that forms Earth's **atmosphere**. Its composition varies slightly from place to place—particularly with regard to the amounts of carbon dioxide and water vapor it contains—but the average composition of dry air is (percentages by volume):

> nitrogen 78.1%
>
> oxygen 20.9%
>
> argon 0.9%
>
> other gases 0.1%

air pressure Pressure at a point in the **atmosphere** of Earth or other planetary body with an atmosphere. *See* **atmospheric pressure**.

albedo Proportion of light reflected diffusely by a surface, especially the proportion of the sun's rays reflected back by clouds, vegetation, etc.

ALGOL

ALGOL Acronym for the high-level computer programming language ALGOrithmic Language, used for manipulating mathematical and scientific data.

algorithm Operation or set of operations that are required to effect a particular calculation or to manipulate data in a certain way, usually to solve a specific problem. The term is commonly used in the context of computer programming.

alpha decay Radioactive disintegration of a substance with the emission of **alpha particles**.

alphanumeric Describing characters or their codes that represent letters of the alphabet or numerals, particularly in computer applications.

alpha particle Particle that is composed of two **protons** and two **neutrons** (and is thus the equivalent of a helium nucleus). It is produced by **radioactive** decay and has little penetrative power. It is sometimes represented as α-particle.

alpha radiation Ionizing radiation consisting of a stream of **alpha particles**.

alternating current (a.c.) Electric **current** that reverses its direction of flow in periodic cycles (measured in **hertz**).

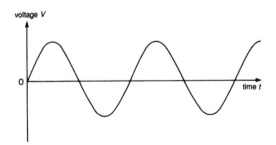

Alternating current varies rapidly with time

alternator Generator that produces alternating current (a.c.) by rotating coils in a magnetic field.

altimeter Instrument for measuring altitude, often a type of **barometer**.

AM Abbreviation of **amplitude modulation**.

ammeter Instrument for measuring electric current, usually calibrated in **amperes**. The common moving-coil ammeter is a type of **galvanometer.**

amorphous Without clear shape or structure.

ampere (A) Basic SI unit of electric **current**.

Ampère's law Relationship that gives the **magnetic induction** at a point due to a given **current** in terms of the current elements and their positions relative to the point. It was named after the French physicist André Marie Ampère. Alternative name: Laplace law.

amplifier Device that can magnify a physical quantity, such as electrical **current** or mechanical force. An electronic amplifier increases the **amplitude** of the input signal, to produce a **gain**.

amplitude Maximum value attained by a quantity that varies in periodic cycles; *i.e.*, the maximum displacement from its mean position, usually equal to half its total displacement.

amplitude modulation (AM) Form of radio transmission used on the long and medium wavebands, in which the information content (the sound being broadcast) is conveyed by variations in the **amplitude** of the **carrier wave**.

amu Abbreviation of **atomic mass unit**.

analog computer Computer that represents numerical values by continuously variable physical quantities (*e.g.*, voltage, current), as opposed to a digital computer.

analog/digital converter Device that converts the output of an **analog computer** into digital signals for a **digital computer**.

anchor ring Alternative name for **torus**.

AND gate Computer logic element that combines two binary input signals to produce one output signal according to particular rules. Alternative name: AND element.

anechoic Without echo. The term usually describes any structure, or room, that has been lined with sound-absorbent material so that sound reflection is reduced to a minimum.

anemometer Instrument for measuring the speed of wind.

angle of incidence Angle that a ray or any other straight line makes with the normal to a surface at which it arrives.

angle of reflection Angle made by a ray with the normal to a surface from which it is reflected at the point of reflection.

angle of refraction Angle made by a ray refracted at a surface separating two media with the normal to the surface at the point of **refraction**.

angstrom (Å) Unit of **wavelength** for **electromagnetic radiation**, including **light** and **X-rays**, equal to 10^{-10}m. It was named after the Swedish physicist A. J. Ångström (1814–1874).

angular frequency Number of vibrations per unit time, multiplied by 2π, of an oscillating body, usually expressed in radians per second. Alternative name: pulsatance.

angular momentum (L) For a rotating object, the cross-product of a **vector** from a specified reference point to a particle and the particle's **linear momentum**.

anion Negatively charged **ion**.

anisotropic Describing a substance that has different properties with respect to velocity of light transmission, conductivity of heat and electricity, and compressibility in different directions of its matrix.

annealing Process of bringing about a desirable change in the properties of a metal or glass (*e.g.*, making it tougher), by heating it to a predetermined temperature, thus altering its microscopic structure.

annihilation Result of a collision between a particle and its **antiparticle**, accompanied by the evolution of energy. After the collision, both particles cease to exist.

anode Positive terminal of an **electrolytic cell** or **thermionic valve**.

antenna Alternative name for an **aerial**.

antimatter Matter that is composed of **antiparticles**.

antiparticle Subatomic particle that corresponds to another particle of equal mass but opposite **electric charge** (*e.g.*, a positron is the antiparticle of the electron).

aperture Effective diameter of a lens or lens system. Its reciprocal is the **f-number**.

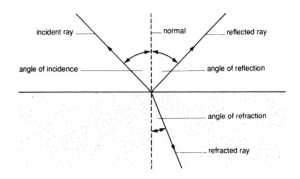

Angles of incidence, reflection and refraction

apparent depth Perceived depth of a liquid, which is different from its actual depth because of the **refraction** of light.

Appleton layer Upper level of the **ionosphere** (at about 200km altitude by day, and at 300km by night), which reflects radio waves in the medium waveband back to Earth. It was named after the British physicist Edward Appleton (1892–1965). Alternative name: F-layer.

applications program Computer **program** written by the user for a specific purpose, *e.g.*, record-keeping or stock control.

Archimedes' principle When a body is immersed in a fluid it has an apparent loss in weight equal to the weight of the fluid it displaces. It was named after the Greek mathematician Archimedes (287?–212 B.C.).

arc lamp Type of lamp that uses an electric arc to generate light.

area Measure of the size of a surface. The areas of some common figures are as follows (where l = length, h = height or altitude, r = radius):

square	l^2
rectangle	lh
parallelogram	lh
triangle	$\frac{1}{2} lh$
circle $\bullet$	πr^2
sphere	$4\pi r^3$
cone	πrs (curved surface, s = slant height) $\pi rs + \pi r^2$ (total surface)
cylinder	$2\pi rh$ (curved surface) $2\pi rh + 2\pi r^2$ (total surface)

arithmetic unit Part or a computer's **central processor** that performs arithmetical operations (addition, subtraction, multiplication, division).

armature 1. Moving part (rotor) of a d.c. electric motor or **generator**. 2. Piece of iron or steel placed across the poles of a permanent magnet in order to preserve its properties. Alternative name: keeper. 3. Moving metallic part that closes a magnetic circuit in an electric bell or relay.

artificial radioactivity Radioactivity in a substance that is not normally radioactive. It is created by bombarding the substance with ionizing **radiation**. Alternative name: induced radioactivity.

astigmatism 1.Vision defect caused by irregular curvature of the lens of the **eye**, so that light does not focus properly. 2. Failure of an optical system, such as a **lens** or a **mirror**, to focus the image of a point as a single point.

astronomical unit (AU) Measure used for distances within the solar system. One astronomical unit is equal to the mean distance between Earth and the sun.

astrophysics Branch of astronomy concerned with the structure, physical properties and behavior of the universe and heavenly bodies within it; *e.g.*, luminosity, size, mass, density, temperature and chemical composition.

atmosphere 1. Air or gases surrounding Earth or other heavenly body. Earth's atmosphere extends outward several thousand miles, becoming increasingly rarefied until it merges gradually into **space**. For composition, *see* **air**. 2. (atm.) Unit of **pressure**, equal to 101,325 pascals (Pa), equivalent to 760 mm Hg.

atmospheric pressure Force exerted on the surface of Earth (and any other planetary body), and on the organisms that live there, by the weight of the atmosphere. Its standard value at sea level is 101,325 pascals, or 760 mm Hg, and it decreases with altitude, but is subject to local and temporary variation. It is measured with a **barometer**.

atom Fundamental particle that is the basic unit of matter. An atom consists of a positively charged **nucleus** surrounded by negatively charged electrons restricted to orbitals of a given energy level. Most of the **mass** of an atom is in the nucleus, which is composed principally of protons (positively charged) and **neutrons** (electrically neutral); hydrogen is exceptional in having merely one proton in its nucleus. The number of electrons is equal to the number of **protons**, and this is the **atomic number**. The chemical behavior of an atom is determined by how many electrons it has, and how they are transferred to, or shared with, other atoms to form chemical bonds. *See also* **atomic mass; Bohr theory; isotope; subatomic particle**.

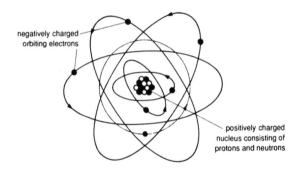

negatively charged orbiting electrons

positively charged nucleus consisting of protons and neutrons

Atom has a central nucleus and orbiting electrons

atomic bomb Explosive device of great power that derives its energy from **nuclear fission**. Alternative names: atom bomb, nuclear bomb.

atomic clock Time-keeping device in which the operation is controlled by an atomic or molecular process. Clocks based on the frequency with which an atom of cesium changes state in a magnetic field are accurate to within one second per 30,000 years.

atomic energy Energy that is released by nuclear fission or **nuclear fusion**. Alternative name: **nuclear energy**.

atomic mass Alternative name for atomic weight. *See* also **relative atomic mass**.

atomic mass unit (amu) Arbitrary unit that is used to express the mass of individual atoms. The standard is a mass equal to 1/12 of the mass of a carbon atom (the carbon-12 **isotope**). A mass expressed on this standard is called a relative atomic mass (r.a.m.), symbol A_r. An alternative name for atomic mass unit is dalton.

atomic number (at. no.) Number equal to the number of **protons** in the nucleus of an atom of a particular element, symbol Z. Alternative name: proton number.

atomic orbital Wave function that characterizes the behavior of an **electron** when orbiting the nucleus of an atom. It can be visualized as the region in space occupied by the electron.

atomic weight (at. wt.) Relative mass of an **atom** given in terms of **atomic mass units**. *See* **relative atomic mass**.

attenuation Loss of strength of a physical quantity (*e.g.,* a radio signal or an electric current) caused by **absorption** or **scattering**.

AU Abbreviation of **astronomical unit**.

Auger effect Radiationless ejection of an **electron** from an **ion**. It is named after the French physicist Pierre Auger (1899–1993). Alternative name: autoionization.

autoionization Spontaneous ionization of excited **atoms, molecules** or fragments of an **ion**. Alternative name: pre-ionization. *See also* **Auger effect**.

autoradiography Technique for photographing a specimen by injecting it with radioactive material so that it produces its own image on a photographic film or plate.

avalanche diode Alternative name for **Zener diode**.

Avogadro constant

Avogadro constant (L) Number of particles (atoms or molecules) in a **mole** of a substance. It has a value of 6.02×10^{23}. It was named after the Italian scientist Amedeo Avogadro (1776–1856). Alternative name: Avogadro's number.

Avogadro's law Under the same conditions of pressure and temperature, equal volumes of all gases contain equal numbers of **molecules.** Alternative name: Avogadro's hypothesis.

Avogadro's number Alternative name for **Avogadro constant.**

avoirdupois System of weights, still used for some purposes in Britain, based on a pound (symbol lb), equivalent to 2.205kg, and subdivided into 16 ounces, or 7,000 grains. In science and medicine it has been almost entirely replaced by **SI units**.

B

back e.m.f. Electromotive force produced in a circuit that opposes the main flow of current; *e.g.*, in an electrolytic cell because of **polarization** or in an electric motor because of **electromagnetic induction**.

background radiation Radiation from natural sources, including outer space (cosmic radiation) and radioactive substances on Earth (*e.g.*, in igneous rocks such as granite).

backing store Computer store that is larger than the main (immediate access) memory, but with a longer access time.

balance Apparatus for weighing things accurately; types include a beam balance, spring balance and substitution balance.

ballistic missile Ground-to-ground missile that moves under gravity after the initial powered and guided stage.

ballistics Study of projectiles moving under the force of gravity only.

Balmer series Visible atomic **spectrum** of hydrogen, consisting of a unique series of energy emission levels that appears as lines of red, blue and blue-violet light. It is the key to the discrete energy levels of electrons (*see* **Bohr theory**).

bar Unit of pressure defined as 10^5 newtons per square meter, or pascals (Pa); equal to approximately one atmosphere.

barometer Instrument for measuring atmospheric pressure, much used in meteorology.

barrel

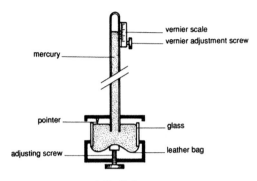

A Fortin barometer

barrel Unit of volume. In the oil industry, 1 barrel = about 159 liters (35 gallons); in brewing, 1 barrel = 32 gallons.

baryon One of a group of subatomic particles that include **protons**, **neutrons** and **hyperons**, and which are involved in strong interaction with other particles.

battery Device for producing electricity (direct current) by chemical action; alternative name: cell. *See* **Daniell cell; dry cell; Leclanché cell; primary cell; secondary cell**. *See also* **fuel cell; solar cell**.

Baumé scale Scale of **relative density (specific gravity)** of liquids, commonly used in continental Europe. It was named after the French chemist Antoine Baumé (1728–1804).

bearing In surveying and telecommunications, horizontal angle between a line and a reference direction, measured clockwise from north.

beats Variation in volume that occurs when two notes of nearly equal frequency sound simultaneously.

Beckman thermometer Mercury thermometer used for accurately measuring very small changes or differences in temperature. The scale usually covers only 6 or 7 degrees. It was named after the German chemist Ernst Beckman (1853–1923).

becquerel (Bq) SI unit of radioactivity, equal to the number of **atoms** of a **radioactive** substance that disintegrate in one second. It was named after the French physicist Henri Becquerel (1852–1908). 1 Bq = 2.7 x 10^{-11} curies (the former unit of radioactivity).

Beer's law Concerned with the absorption of light by substances, it states that the fraction of incident light absorbed by a solution at a given **wavelength** is related to the thickness of the absorbing layer and the concentration of the absorbing substance. Alternative name: Beer-Lambert law.

bel (B) Unit representing the ratio of two amounts of power, *e.g.,* of sound or an electronic signal, equal to 10 **decibels.** It was named after the American inventor Alexander Graham Bell (1847–1922).

beta decay Disintegration of an unstable **radioactive** nucleus that involves the emission of a **beta particle**. It occurs when a neutron emits an electron and is itself converted to a proton, resulting in an increase of one proton in the nucleus concerned and a corresponding decrease of one neutron. This leads to the formation of a different element (*e.g.,* beta decay of the radio-isotope carbon-14 produces nitrogen and an electron).

beta particle High-velocity electron emitted by a **radioactive** nucleus undergoing **beta decay**. It is sometimes represented as β-particle.

beta radiation Radiation, consisting of beta particles (electrons), due to **beta decay**.

biconcave Describing a lens that is concave on both surfaces.

biconvex Describing a lens that is convex on both surfaces.

billion Number now generally accepted as being equivalent to 1,000 million (10^9). Formerly in Britain a billion was regarded as a million million (10^{12}).

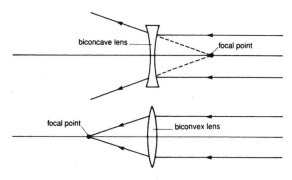

Biconvex and biconcave lenses

bimetallic strip Strip consisting of two metals with different thermal expansions jointed together, which as a result bends when heated; used in **thermostats**.

binding energy Energy required to cause a **nucleus** to decompose into its constituent **neutrons** and **protons**.

biophysics Use of ideas and methods of **physics** in the study of living organisms and processes.

bistable circuit Alternative name for a **flip-flop**.

bit Amount of information that is required to express choice between two possibilities. The term is commonly applied to a single digit of binary notation in a computer. The word is an abbreviation of *binary digit*, either 1 or 0, the only two digits in binary notation.

black body Hypothetical full or complete absorber and radiator of **radiation**.

blind spot In radio, an area within the normal range of radio transmission where reception is poor. The low field strength is usually caused by an interference pattern produced by man-made obstructions or geographical features.

blink microscope Instrument for comparing two very similar photographs, *e.g.*, of stars or bacteria. The photographs are viewed side by side, one with each eye, and are rapidly concealed and uncovered. The brain's attempts to superimpose the two images reveals any slight differences between them.

Bohr theory Atomic theory that assumes all **atoms** are made up of a central positively charged **nucleus** surrounded by orbiting planetary **electrons**, and which incorporates a **quantum theory** to limit the number of allowed **orbitals** in which the electrons can move. Each orbital has a characteristic energy level, and emission of electromagnetic radiation (*e.g.*, light) occurs when an electron jumps to an orbital at a lower energy level (see **Balmer series**). It was named after the Danish physicist Niels Bohr (1885–1962).

boiling point (b.p.) Temperature at which a liquid freely turns into a vapor; the **vapor pressure** of the liquid then equals the external pressure on it.

Boltzmann constant (*k*) Equal to R/L = 1.3806 x 10^{-23} J K^{-1} (joule per Kelvin), where R = **gas constant** and L = **Avogadro constant**. It was named after the Austrian physicist Ludwig Boltzmann (1844–1906).

bomb calorimeter Apparatus for measuring the heat energy released during the combustion of a substance (such as a fuel).

Bose-Einstein statistics Statistical mechanics of systems of identical particles that have their wave functions unaltered if any two particles are interchanged.

boson Subatomic particle, *e.g.*, **alpha particle**, **photon**, that obeys **Bose-Einstein statistics** but does not obey the **Pauli exclusion principle**. Atomic **nuclei** of even mass numbers are also bosons.

boundary layer Disturbed region that forms around any surface moving through a fluid; the transitional zone throughout which the surface affects the motion of the fluid.

Bourdon gauge Instrument for measuring fluid **pressure** that consists of a coiled flattened tube that tends to straighten when pressure inside it increases. The movement of the end of the tube is made to work a pointer that moves around a scale. It was named after the French engineer Eugène Bourdon (1808–1884).

Boyle's law At constant temperature the volume of a gas V is inversely proportional to its pressure p; *i.e.*, pV = a constant. It was named after the Irish chemist Robert Boyle (1627–1691).

Bragg's law When **X-rays** are refracted by the layers of atoms in a crystal, the maximum intensity of the refracted ray occurs when $\sin\theta = n\lambda/2d$, where d = distance separating the layers, θ = complement of the **angle of incidence**, n = an integer and λ = **wavelength** of the X-rays. It was named after the British physicist William Henry Bragg (1862–1942).

breakdown diode Alternative name for **Zener diode**.

breeder reactor Nuclear reactor that produces more fissile material (*e.g.*, plutonium) than it consumes.

Brewster's law The tangent of the angle of **polarization** of light by a substance is equal to the **refractive index** of the substance. It was named after the British physicist David Brewster (1781–1868).

British Thermal Unit (Btu) Amount of heat required to raise the temperature of 1 pound of water through $1°$F. 1 Btu = 1,055 joules.

Brownian movement Random motion of particles of a **solid** suspended in a **liquid** or **gas**, caused by collisions with molecules of the suspending medium. It was named after the British botanist Robert Brown (1773–1858). Alternative name: Brownian motion.

bubble chamber A container of pressurized liquid hydrogen at just above its normal boiling point, used to reveal the tracks of charged subatomic particles. As particles pass through the chamber, the pressure is suddenly lowered so that local boiling of the hydrogen produces a series of small bubbles along the particles' ionized tracks. *See also* **cloud chamber**.

bulk modulus Elastic modulus equal to the pressure on an object divided by its fractional decrease in volume. It is the ratio pV/v where p = intensity of stress, V = volume of the substance before pressure was applied, and v is the change in volume produced by the stress.

buoyancy Result of **upthrust** on an object floating or suspended in a fluid. *See* **Archimedes' principle**.

byte Single unit of information in a **computer,** usually a group of 8 **bits**.

C

cesium clock Atomic clock used in the **SI unit** definition of the second.

calibration 1. Measuring scale on a scientific instrument or apparatus. 2. Method of putting a scale on a scientific instrument, usually by checking it against fixed quantities or standards.

calliper Measuring instrument that resembles a large pair of geometrical dividers; there are internal and external versions.

calomel half-cell Reference **electrode** of known potential consisting of mercury, mercury(I) chloride and potassium chloride solution. Alternative names: calomel electrode, calomel reference electrode.

calorie Amount of heat required to raise the temperature of 1 kg of water by 1°C at one atmosphere pressure; equal to 4.184 joules. *See also* **Calorie**.

Calorie Amount of heat required to raise the temperature of 1 kg of water by 1°C at one atmosphere pressure; equal to 4.184 kilojoules. It is used as a unit of energy of food (when it is sometimes spelled with a small c). Alternative name: kilocalorie, large calorie. *See also* **calorie**.

calorific value Quantity of heat liberated on the complete combustion of a unit weight or unit volume of fuel.

calorimeter Apparatus for measuring heat quantities generated in or evolved by materials in processes such as chemical reactions, changes of state and solvation.

candela Unit of luminous intensity.

candle power (cp) Luminous intensity expressed in candles.

capacitance (C) Ratio of the charge on one of the conductors of a **capacitor** (there being an equal and an opposite charge on the other conductor) to the potential difference between them. The SI unit of capacitance is the farad.

capacitor Device that can store charge and introduces **capacitance** into an electrical circuit. Alternative names: condenser, electrical condenser.

capillarity In physics, a phenomenon—resulting from **surface tension**—that causes low-density liquids to flow along narrow (capillary) tubes or soak into porous materials. Alternative name: capillary action.

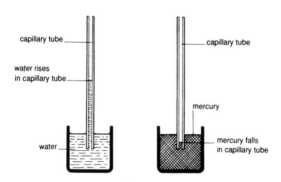

Capillarity causes liquids to rise or fall

capillary Any narrow tube, in which **capillarity** can occur.

carburetor Part of an internal combustion engine, in which air and liquid hydrocarbon fuel are mixed and vaporized.

card punch Machine for punching coded sets of holes in punched cards, to be fed through a **card reader** for inputting **data** into a computer.

card reader Computer **input device** that reads **data** off punched cards.

Carnot cycle Reversible cycle of four operations that occur in a perfect heat engine. These operations are isothermal expansion (*see* **isothermal process**), adiabatic expansion (*see* **adiabatic process**), isothermal compression and adiabatic compression. Carnot's principle states that the efficiency of a perfect heat engine depends on the temperature range in which it works, and not on the properties of the substances with which it works. It was named after the French physicist Nicolas Carnot (1796–1832).

carrier wave In radio, the continuously transmitted radio wave whose amplitude or frequency is modulated by a signal representing the sound being broadcast. *See also* **amplitude modulation; frequency modulation.**

cathode Negatively charged electrode in an **electrolytic cell** or **battery**.

cathode-ray oscilloscope (CRO) Apparatus based on a **cathode-ray tube** that provides a visible image of one or more rapidly varying electrical signals.

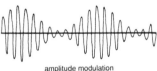

amplitude modulation

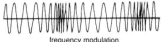

frequency modulation

A radio carrier wave is modulated

cathode rays Stream of **electrons** produced by the **cathode** (negative electrode) of an evacuated **discharge tube** (such as a **cathode-ray tube**).

cathode-ray tube Vacuum tube that allows the direct observation of the behavior of cathode rays. It is used as the picture tube in television receivers and in cathode-ray oscilloscopes.

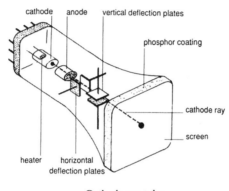

Cathode-ray tube

cation Positively charged **ion**, which travels toward the **cathode** during **electrolysis**.

cell Alternative name for an **electrolytic cell**.

Celsius scale Temperature scale on which the **freezing point** of pure water is 0°C and the **boiling point** is 100°C. A degree Celsius is equal to a unit on the **kelvin** scale. To convert a Celsius temperature to kelvin, add 273.16 (and omit the degree sign). To convert a Celsius temperature to a Fahrenheit one, multiply by 9/5 and add 32. It is named after the Swedish astronomer Anders Celsius (1701–1744).

centigrade scale Former name for the **Celsius scale**.

central processor Heart of a **digital computer** that controls and coordinates all the other activities of the machine, and performs logical processes on **data** loaded into it according to **program** instructions it holds.

center of curvature Geometric center of a spherical mirror.

center of mass Point at which the whole **mass** of an object may be considered to be concentrated. Alternative name: center of gravity.

centrifugal force Apparent (but not real) outward force on any object moving in a circular path. *See also* **centripetal force**.

centrifuge Instrument used for the separation of substances through sedimentation by rotation at high speeds. *E.g.,* the separation of components of cells. Sedimentation varies according to the size of the component.

centripetal force Force, directed toward the center, that causes a body to move in a circular path. For an object of mass m moving with a speed v in a curve of radius of curvature r, it is equal to mv^2/r.

Cerenkov counter Method of measuring radioactivity by utilizing the effect of **Cerenkov radiation**.

Cerenkov radiation Light emitted when charged particles pass through a transparent medium at a velocity that is greater than that of light in the medium. It was named after the Soviet physicist Pavel Cerenkov (1904–1990).

c.g.s unit Centimeter-gram-second unit, in general scientific use before the adoption of SI units.

chain reaction Nuclear or chemical reaction in which the products ensure that the reaction continues (*e.g.,* nuclear fission, combustion).

charge *See* **electric charge**.

Charles' law At a given pressure, the volume of an ideal gas is directly proportional to its absolute temperature. It was named after the French physicist Jacques Charles (1746–1823).

chromatic aberration *See* **aberration**.

circuit breaker Safety device in an electric circuit that interrupts the current flow in the event of a fault. *See* also **fuse**.

classical physics Physics prior to the introduction of **quantum theory** and a knowledge of **relativity**.

cloud chamber Apparatus for observing the tracks of subatomic particles. It consists of a chamber containing a liquid (such as ethanol) and its saturated vapor. Sudden expansion of the chamber (by retracting one wall) lowers the temperature, so that droplets of liquid condense from the now supersaturated vapor onto ions along the tracks of the particles. *See* also **bubble chamber**.

COBOL Acronym of Common Business Oriented Language, a computer programming language designed for commercial use.

Cockcroft-Walton generator High-voltage **direct current** generator used for accelerating nuclear particles to high speeds. It was named after the British scientist John Cockcroft (1897–1967) and the Irish physicist Ernest Walton (1903–1995).

coefficient Number or parameter that measures some specified property of a given substance; *e.g.,* coefficient of friction, coefficient of viscosity.

coherent units System of units in which the desired units are obtained by multiplying or dividing base units, with no numerical constant involved. *See also* **SI units.**

cohesion Attraction between similar particles (atoms or molecules of the same substance); *e.g.,* between water molecules to create **surface tension**. *See also* **adhesion**.

colloid

colloid Form of matter that consists of small particles, about 10^{-4} to 10^{-6} mm across, dispersed in a medium such as air or water. Common colloids include **aerosols** (*e.g.*, fog, mist) and **gels** (*e.g.*, gelatin, rubber). A non-colloidal substance is termed a crystalloid.

color Visual sensation or perception that results from the adsorption of light energy of a particular **wavelength** by the cones of the retina of the eye. There are two or more types of cone, each of which are sensitive to different wavelengths of light. The brain combines nerve impulses from these cones to produce the perception of color. The color of an object thus depends on the wavelength of light it reflects (other wavelengths being absorbed) or transmits.

colorimeter Instrument for measuring the color intensity of a medium such as a colored solution (which can be related to concentration and therefore provide a method of quantitative analysis). The technique is termed colorimetry.

communications satellite Man-made object that orbits Earth, used for relaying radio, television and telephone signals. Many such satellites are in **geostationary orbits**.

commutator Device for altering or reversing the direction of an electric current, *e.g.*, on a d.c. electric motor.

compass Apparatus for finding direction (parallel to Earth's surface), usually by alignment with Earth's magnetic field. In its simplest form, it consists of a magnetized needle pivoted horizontally at its center. Such magnetic compasses are affected by nearby magnetic materials and electrical equipment, and have to be corrected for the continuous slow movement of the position of the north magnetic pole. A gyrocompass overcomes these problems by using a **gyroscope** with its axis permanently aligned with north.

compiler Computer **program** that converts a source language into machine code (readable by the computer).

compound pendulum Vertical bar or rod pivoted at the top and with a weight near the bottom. If its center of mass is a distance h from the pivot and the **radius of gyration** is k, the period of swing t is given by $t = 2\pi (h^2 + k^2) / hg]^{1/2}$, where g is the acceleration of free fall.

Compton effect Reduction in the energy of a photon as a result of its interaction with a free electron. Some of the photon's energy is transferred to the electron. It was named after the American physicist Arthur Compton (1892–1962).

computer Electronic device that can accept **data**, apply a series of logical operations to it (obeying a **program**), and supply the results of these operations. *See* **analog computer**; **digital computer**.

concave Describing a surface that curves inward (as opposed to one that is convex).

condensation Change of a gas or vapor into a liquid or solid by cooling.

condensation pump Alternative name for **diffusion pump**.

condenser 1. In electricity, an alternative name for a **capacitor**. 2. In optics, a lens or mirror that concentrates a light source.

conductance Ability to convey energy as heat or electricity. Electrical conductance, measured in siemens, is the reciprocal of **resistance**. Alternative name: conductivity

conduction, electrical Passage of electricity by materials.

conduction, thermal Transmission of heat by materials.

conduction band Energy range in a **semiconductor** within which **electrons** can be made to flow by an applied **electric field**.

conductivity, electrical Measure of the ability of a substance to conduct electricity, the reciprocal of **resistivity**. It is measured in ohms^{-1} m^{-1}. *See also* **conductance**.

conductivity, thermal Thermal conducting power of a material.

conductor 1. Material that allows heat to flow through it by **conduction**. 2. Material that allows electricity to flow through it; a conductor has a low **resistance**.

configuration Arrangement of electrons about the nucleus of an atom. Alternative name: electron configuration.

conservation of energy Law that states that in all processes occurring in an isolated system the energy of the system remains constant. *See also* **thermodynamics, laws of**.

conservation of mass Principle that states that the products of a purely chemical reaction have the same total mass as the reactants.

conservation of momentum Law that states that the total momentum of two colliding objects before impact is equal to their total momentum after impact.

constant Quantity that remains the same in all circumstances. *E.g.*, the acceleration of free fall is a physical constant; in the expression $2y = 5x^2$, the numbers 2 and 5 are constants (and x and y are variables).

continuous stationery Long length of fan-folded paper with sprocket holes down each side for transporting it through a computer printer. The paper may be perforated to facilitate tearing off the sprocket holes and for tearing the paper into single sheets after printing.

continuous wave Electromagnetic wave of constant **amplitude**.

control rod Length of material that is a good absorber of **thermal neutrons**, used to control the **chain reaction** in a **nuclear reactor**.

convection Transport of **heat** by the movement of the heated substance (usually a fluid such as air or water).

converging lens Lens capable of bringing light to a focus; a convex lens.

core Element in a computer **memory** consisting of a piece of magnetic material that can retain a permanent positive or negative electric charge until a current passes through it (when it changes polarity).

cosmic radiation Radiation of extremely short wavelength (about 10^{-15} m) from outer space. *See also* **cosmic rays**.

cosmic rays Radiation consisting of high-energy particles from outer space. Primary rays consist of **protons** and nuclei as well as other subatomic particles. Collision with nitrogen and oxygen atoms in the atmosphere generates secondary cosmic rays, consisting of elementary particles and **gamma rays**.

coulomb (C) SI unit of electric charge, defined as the quantity of electricity transported by a current of 1 ampere in 1 second. It was named after the French physicist Charles Coulomb (1736–1806).

counter 1. In physics, electronic apparatus for detecting and counting particles, usually by making them generate pulses of electric current; the actual counting circuit is a **scaler**. 2. In computing, any device that accumulates totals (*e.g.,* of repeated program loops or cards passing through a punched **card reader**).

couple In physics, a pair of equal and parallel forces acting in opposite directions upon an object. This produces a turning effect (**torque**) equal to one of the forces times the distance between them.

coupling In physics, connection between two oscillating systems.

critical angle In optics, smallest angle of incidence at which **total internal reflection** occurs.

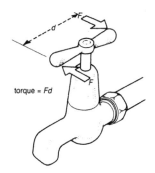

A simple tap uses a couple

critical mass Minimum amount of fissile material required to maintain a nuclear **chain reaction** (*see* **nuclear fission**).

critical pressure Pressure necessary to condense a substance at its **critical temperature**.

critical state Conditions of temperature and pressure at which the liquid and gas phases become one phase—*i.e.*, they have the same density.

critical temperature 1. Temperature above which a gas cannot be liquefied (no matter how high the pressure). 2. Temperature at which a magnetic material loses its magnetism. Alternative name: Curie point.

critical volume Volume of one unit of mass of a substance at its **critical pressure** and **critical temperature**.

CRO Abbreviation of **cathode-ray oscilloscope**.

cryogenics Branch of physics that involves low temperatures and their effects.

crystal Solid that has a definite regular shape. Crystals of the same substance have the same specific shapes, reflecting the way its component atoms or ions are regularly arranged in a lattice. *See also* **liquid crystal**.

crystal lattice Regular arrangement of atoms or ions in a **crystal**.

crystalline Having the form of crystals, as opposed to being **amorphous**.

crystallography Study of crystals.

crystalloid Substance that is not a **colloid** and can therefore pass through a semipermeable membrane.

curie (Ci) Measure of radioactivity. 1 Ci = 3.700 x 10^{10} disintegrations per second. It was named after the Polish-born French scientist Marie Curie (1867–1934). It has been replaced in **SI units** by the **becquerel**.

Curie point Temperature above which a magnetic material loses its **magnetism**. Alternative name: critical temperature.

Curie's law In a **paramagnetic** substance, the **magnetic susceptibility** is inversely proportional to the **absolute temperature**.

current, electric Flow of electrons along a conductor, measured in **amperes**.

cycle One of a repeating series of similar changes; *e.g.*, in a wave motion or vibration. One cycle is equal to the period of the motion; the number of cycles per unit time is its frequency. A frequency of 1 cycle per second = 1 **hertz**.

cyclotron Machine for accelerating atomic particles to high speeds. Particles follow a spiral path in a magnetic field between two D-shaped electrodes.

D

dalton Alternative name for **atomic mass unit.**

Dalton's atomic theory Theory that states that matter consists of tiny particles (atoms), and that all the atoms of a particular **element** are exactly alike, but different from the atoms of other elements in behavior and mass. The theory also states that chemical action takes place as a result of attraction between atoms, but it fails to account satisfactorily for the volume relationships that exist between combining gases. It was proposed by the British scientist John Dalton (1766–1844).

Dalton's law of partial pressures In a mixture of gases, the pressure exerted by one of the component gases is the same as if it alone occupied the total volume.

Daniel cell Electrolytic cell that consists of a zinc **half-cell** and a copper half-cell, usually arranged as a zinc **cathode** and a copper **anode** dipping into an **electrolyte** of dilute sulphuric acid.

daraf Unit of the elastance of an electrical component; it is the reciprocal of **capacitance** (the word is **farad** backward).

data Collection of information, often referring to results of a statistical study or to information supplied to, processed by or provided by a computer (excluding the **program**).

data bank Large file of computer **data,** usually accessible (to many users) by direct access.

database 1. Organized collection of **data** that is held on a computer, where it is regularly updated and can easily be accessed. 2. **Applications program** that controls and makes use of a database.

data transmission Transfer of **data** between outstations and a central **computer** or between different computer systems.

daughter element One of the elements produced when an atom divides by **nuclear fission**.

daughter nucleus New atomic nucleus produced when the nucleus of a radio-isotope decays.

d.c. Abbreviation of **direct current**.

de Brogile wavelength Wavelength of a wave that is associated with the motion of a particle. For a particle of mass m moving with speed v, the wavelength of the wave is given by $\lambda = h / mv$, where h is **Planck's constant**. It is named after the French physicist Louis de Broglie (1892–1987).

debug To remove a bug from a computer system.

Debye-Hückel theory Theory that explains variations from the ideal behavior of **electrolytes** in terms of inter-ionic attraction, and assumes that electrolytes in solution are completely dissociated into charged ions. It was named after the physicists Peter Debye (1884–1966) and Erich Hückel (1896–1980).

deca Prefix denoting 10 times in the metric system.

decay Breakdown, through **radioactivity**, of a radioactive substance. Such decay is typically exponential. *See also* **half-life**.

decibel Unit used for comparing power levels (on a logarithmic scale); one-tenth of a bel. It is commonly used in comparison of sound intensity. *See also* **bel**.

decimal system Number system that uses the base 10; *i.e.*, it uses the digits 1 to 9 and 0.

declination Alternative term for **magnetic declination**.

degaussing Process of demagnetizing a metal object, *e.g.*, a ship, by encircling it with an **electric field**.

degradation In physics, the irreversible loss of energy available to do work.

degree 1. Unit of difference used in temperature scales. 2. Unit derived by dividing a circle into 360 segments, used to measure angles and describe direction; it is subdivided into minutes and seconds (of arc). Both types of degrees have the symbol °.

degree of freedom One of several variable factors, *e.g.*, temperature, pressure and concentration, that must be made constant for the condition of a system at equilibrium to be defined.

delocalization Phenomenon that occurs in certain molecules, *e.g.*, benzene. Some of the electrons involved in chemical bonding the atoms are not restricted to one particular bond, but are free to move between two or more bonds. The electrical conductivity of metals is due to the presence of delocalized electrons.

delta ray Electron that is ejected from an atom when it is struck by a high-energy particle.

demagnetization Removal of the **magnetism** from a ferromagnetic material (*e.g.*, by using a diminishing alternating current field or merely by striking it).

demodulation Process by which information is extracted and sorted from the **carrier wave** of a radio broadcast. *See* **amplitude modulation; frequency modulation**.

dendrite In crystallography, a branching **crystal**, such as occurs in some rocks and minerals.

density 1. Mass of unit volume of a substance. For an object of mass m and volume V, the density d is m/V. It is commonly expressed in units gm cm^{-3} (although the SI unit is kg m^{-3}). 2. Number of items in a defined surface area or volume (*e.g.*, charge density, population density).

depolarization Removal or prevention of electrical polarity or **polarization**.

depression of freezing point Reduction of the **freezing point** of a liquid when a solid is dissolved in it. At constant pressure and for dilute solutions of a nonvolatile solvent, the depression of the freezing point is directly proportional to the concentration of the solutes.

desktop publishing (DTP) Technique that uses a **microcomputer** linked to a **word processor** (with access to various type fonts and justification programs) and a laser **printer** to produce multiple copies of a document that rivals conventional printing in quality. The addition of a scanner allows the introduction of simple graphics (illustrations).

desorption Reverse process to **adsorption**.

deuterium One of the three **isotopes** of hydrogen, with one proton and one neutron in its atomic nucleus. Its oxide, deuterium oxide, is also known as heavy water. It has a relative atomic mass of 2.0141. Alternative name: heavy hydrogen.

deuteron Positively charged particle that is composed of one **neutron** and one **proton**; it is the nucleus of a **deuterium** atom. Deuterons are often used to bombard other particles inside a **cyclotron**.

deviation Error in a compass reading caused by nearby magnetic disturbances.

Dewar flask Double-walled container that has a vacuum between the two walls in order to reduce heat transmission by **conduction** or **convection**. The walls are usually silvered to minimize transmission by radiation. It was named after the British scientist James Dewar (1842–1923). Alternative name: vacuum flask.

dew point Temperature to which air must be cooled in order for it to become saturated with water vapor, which then condenses as mist or dew. Alternative name: dew temperature.

dextrorotatory Describing an **optically active** compound that causes the plane of polarized light to rotate in a clockwise direction. It is indicated by the prefix (+)- or *d*-.

dialysis Separation of **colloids** from **crystalloids** using selective diffusion through a semipermeable membrane. It is the process by which globular proteins can be separated from low-molecular-weight solutes, as in filtering ("purifying") blood in an artificial kidney machine: the membrane retains protein molecules and allows small solute molecules and water to pass through.

diamagnetism Phenomenon in which magnetic susceptibility is negative, *i.e.*, repelled by a magnet.

diaphragm A thin membrane that vibrates in response to, or to produce, sound waves, *e.g.*, the cone in a loudspeaker.

dichroism Property of a few substances that makes them transmit some colors and reflect others, or which display certain colors when viewed from one angle and different colors when viewed from another.

dielectric Nonconductor of electricity in which an electric field persists in the presence of an inducing field. A dielectric is the insulating material in a **capacitor.**

dielectric constant Alternative name for relative **permittivity**.

dielectric strength Property of an **insulator** that enables it to withstand electric stress without breaking down.

dielectrophoresis Movement of electrically polarized particles in a variable **electric field.**

differentiator Analog computer device whose (variable) output is proportional to the time differential of the (variable) input.

diffraction Bending of the path of a beam (*e.g.*, of light or electrons) at the edge of an object.

diffraction grating Optical device that is used for producing **spectra**. It consists of a sheet of glass or plastic marked with closely spaced parallel lines (as many as 10,000 per centimeter). The spectra are produced by a combination of **diffraction** and **interference**.

diffusion of gases Phenomenon by which gases mix together, reducing any concentration gradient to zero; *e.g.*, in gas exchange between plant leaves and air.

diffusion of light Spreading or scattering of light.

diffusion of solutions Free movement of **molecules** or **ions** of a dissolved substance through a solvent, resulting in complete mixing. *See also* **osmosis**.

diffusion pump Apparatus used to produce a high vacuum. The pump employs mercury or oil at low vapor-pressure that carries along in its flow molecules of a gas from a low pressure established by a backing pump. Alternative names: condensation pump, vacuum pump.

digital/analog converter Device that converts digital signals into continuosly variable electrical signals for use by an **analog computer**.

digital computer Computer that operates on **data** supplied and stored in digital or number form.

digital display Display that shows readings of a measuring machine, clock, etc. by displaying numerals.

dimension Power to which fundamental unit is raised in a derived unit; *e.g.*, acceleration has the dimensions of $[LT^{-2}]$, *i.e.*, +1 for length and –2 for time, equivalent to length divided by the square of time.

dimensional analysis Prediction of the relationship of quantities. If an equation is correct the **dimensions** of the quantities on each side must be identical. It is an important way of checking the validity of an equation.

diode 1. Electron tube (valve) containing two electrodes, an anode and a cathode. 2. **Rectifier** made up of a **semiconductor** crystal with two terminals.

diopter Unit that is used to express the power of a lens. It is the reciprocal of the **focal length** of the lens in meters. The power of a convergent lens with a focal length of one meter is said to be +1 diopter. The power of a divergent lens is given a negative value.

dip Angle measured in a vertical plane between the direction of Earth's **magnetic field** and the horizontal. Alternative name: magnetic dip.

dipole 1. Pair of equal and opposite electric charges at a (short) distance from each other. 2. Simple type of radio aerial (antenna) consisting of a pair of horizontal or vertical metal rods in line, the signal being picked up at their adjacent ends.

dipole moment Product of one charge of a **dipole** and the distance between the charges.

direct current (d.c.) **Electric current** that flows always in the same direction (as opposed to **alternating current**).

discharge 1. High-voltage "spark" (current flow) between points of large potential difference (*e.g.*, lightning). 2. Removal of the charge between the plates of a **capacitor** by allowing current to flow out of it. 3. Removal of energy from an **electrolytic cell** (battery or accumulator) by allowing current to flow out of it. 4. Process by which **ions** are converted to neutral atoms at an electrode during **electrolysis** (by gain or loss of electrons).

discharge tube Evacuated or gas-filled tube with sealed-in **electrodes** between which a high-voltage electric **discharge** takes place. *See also* **Geissler tube**.

disintegration Breakup of an atomic nucleus either through bombardment by subatomic particles or through radioactive **decay**.

disintegration constant Probability of a radioactive **decay** of an atomic nucleus per unit time. Alternative names: decay constant, transformation constant.

disk Magnetic disk used to record data in computers. *See also* **floppy disk; hard disk**.

diskette Alternative name for a **floppy disk**.

dislocation Imperfection in a **crystal** lattice.

dispersion Splitting of an electromagnetic radiation (*e.g.*, visible light) into its component **wavelengths** when it passes through a medium (because different wavelengths undergo different degrees of **diffraction** or **refraction**).

display Short name for a **liquid-crystal display** (LCD) or a **visual display unit** (VDU).

distance ratio Alternative name for **velocity ratio**.

distillation Method for purification or separation of liquids by heating to the **boiling point**, condensing the vapor, and collecting the distillate. Formerly, the method was used to produce distilled water for chemical experiments and processes that required water to be much purer than in the main water supply. In this application distillation has been largely superseded by ion exchange.

distortion Change from the ideal shape of an object or image, or in the form of a wave pattern (*e.g.*, an electrical signal).

diverging lens Lens that spreads out a beam of light passing through it, often a **concave** lens.

D-lines Pair of characteristic lines in the yellow region of the spectrum of sodium, used as standards in spectroscopy.

domain In a **ferromagnetic** substance, a microscopic region in which atomic **magnetic moments** can be aligned to give it permanent **magnetism**.

donor In physics, an element that donates electrons to form an *n*-type **semiconductor**; *e.g.*, antimony or arsenic may be donor elements for germanium or silicon. *See also* **doping**.

doping Adding of impurity atoms to *e.g.*, germanium or silicon to make them into **semiconductors**. Doping with an element of valency 5 (*e.g.*, antimony, arsenic, phosphorus) donates electrons to form an *n*-type semiconductor; doping with an element of valency 3 (*e.g.*, aluminium, boron, gallium) donates "holes" to form a *p*-type semiconductor.

Doppler effect Phenomenon in which the wavelength of a wave (electromagnetic or sound) changes because its source is moving relative to the observer. If the source is approaching the observer, the wavelength decreases and the frequency increases (*e.g.*, sound rises in pitch). If the source is receding, the wavelength increases and the frequency decreases (*e.g.*, sound falls in pitch, or light shifts toward the red end of the spectrum). The effect is used in astronomy (called red shift) and in Doppler **radars**, which distinguish between moving objects and stationary ones. It was named after the Austrian physicist Christian Doppler (1803–1853).

dosimeter Instrument that measures the dose of **radiation** received by a person or an area.

double refraction Phenomenon shown by certain crystals (*e.g.*, calcite) that splits an incident ray of light into two refracted rays (termed ordinary and extraordinary rays) polarized at right angles to each other. Alternative name: birefringence.

dry cell Electrolytic cell containing no free liquid **electrolyte**. A moist paste of ammonium chloride (NH_4Cl) often acts as electrolyte. Dry cells are used in batteries for flashlights, portable radios, etc.

ductile Describing a substance that exhibits **ductility**.

ductility Property of a metal that allows it to be drawn out into a wire; *e.g.*, copper and silver are very ductile metals.

Duralumin Strong **alloy** of aluminium containing 4% copper and traces of magnesium, manganese and silicon, much used in the aerospace industry.

dynamics Branch of **mechanics** that deals with the actions of forces on objects in motion.

dynamo Device for converting mechanical energy into electrical energy in the form of direct current (d.c.). It consists of conducting coils that rotate between the poles of a powerful magnet.

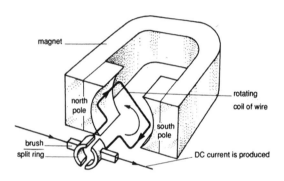

Principle of the dynamo

dyne Force that gives an object of mass 1 gram an acceleration of 1 cm^{-2}. The SI unit of force is the **newton**, equal to 10^5 dynes.

E

earth In electric circuits, a connection to a piece of metal that is in turn linked to Earth. It has the effect of preventing any earthed apparatus from retaining an **electric charge**.

Earth's magnetism *See* **dip; magnetic north; magnetic pole; magnetic storm.**

echo Sound or **electromagnetic radiation** that is reflected or refracted, so that it is delayed and received as a signal distinct from that directly transmitted and it apparently comes from a different direction.

echolocation Method of estimating the location of something by transmitting high-frequency sounds and detecting their echoes. It is the basic of **sonar**.

echo sounder Device for estimating the depth of sea beneath a vessel by measuring the time taken for an ultrasound impulse to reach the sea bed and for its **echo** to return to a receiver. *See also* **sonar**.

eclipse Interception of the light of one heavenly body by another. In a solar eclipse, the light of the sun is blocked out by the intervention of the moon. In a lunar eclipse, Earth moves between the moon and the sun so that the moon reflects no sunlight and does not shine. When the light-emitting body is not totally obscured, it is termed a partial eclipse (as opposed to a total eclipse).

eddy current Electric current within a conductor caused by **electromagnetic induction**. Such currents result in losses of energy in electrical machines (*e.g.*, a transformer, in which they are overcome by laminating the core), but are utilized in induction heating and some braking systems.

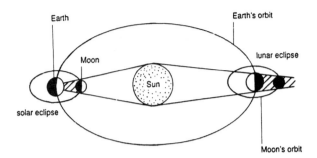

Lunar and solar eclipses

Edison accumulator Alternative name for **nickel-iron accumulator.**

effective resistance Total alternating current resistance of a conductor of electricity.

efficiency Ratio of usable energy output to energy input of a machine, generally expressed as a percentage. For a simple machine it is the ratio of the **mechanical advantage** (force ratio) to the **velocity ratio** (distance ratio).

effort In a simple machine (*e.g.*, lever, pulley) the force that is applied to move a load. The ratio of the load to the effort is the **mechanical advantage** (force ratio).

effusion Passage of gases under pressure through small holes.

elasticity Property of a material that makes it resume its original shape after a deforming force acting upon it is removed. But beyond the **elastic limit**, permanent deformation occurs.

elastic limit A stress applied to an elastic material produces a proportional strain (*see* **Hooke's law**) up to a point, after which the slightest increase in stress produces a large strain (the material becomes plastic) and permanent deformation. That point is the elastic limit.

elastic modulus Ration of stress to strain for an elastic material below its **elastic limit**. *See also* **bulk modulus; Hooke's law; rigidity modulus; Young's modulus.**

elastomer

elastomer Substance that returns to its original shape when stress is removed. *See* **elasticity**.

E-layer Alternative name for the **Heaviside layer**.

electrical condenser Alternative name for **capacitor**.

electrical line of force Line radiating from an **electric field**.

electric arc Luminous discharge produced by the passage of high-voltage electricity between two **electrodes**.

electric charge Excess or deficiency of electrons in an object, giving rise to an overall positive or negative electric charge respectively.

electric current Drift of electrons through a conductor in the same direction, usually because there is a **potential difference** across it.

electric displacement Electric charge per unit area, in coulombs per square meter ($C\ m^{-2}$). Alternative name: electric flux density.

electric field Region surrounding an **electric charge** in which a charged particle is subjected to a force.

electric flux Lines of force that make up an **electric field**.

electricity 1. Branch of science that is concerned with all phenomena caused by static or dynamic electric charges. 2. Supply of electric current.

electric meter Instrument for measuring the consumption of main electricity (in terms of watt-hours, or units).

electric motor Device that converts electrical energy into mechanical energy. A simple electric motor consists of a current-carrying coil that rotates in the magnetic field between the poles of a permanent magnet. *See also* **induction motor; linear motor**.

electric polarization Difference between the displacement of charge and the electric field strength in a **dielectric**.

electrode 1. Conducting plate (anode or cathode) that collects or emits electrons from an **electrolyte** during **electrolysis.** 2. Conducting plate in an **electrolytic cell** (battery), discharge tube or vacuum tube.

electrode potential Electric potential developed by a substance in equilibrium with a solution of its ions.

electrodialysis Removal of salts from a solution (often a **colloid**) by placing the solution between two semipermeable membranes, outside which are electrodes in pure solvent.

electrokinetic potential Alternative name for **zeta potential**.

electrokinetics Branch of science concerned with the study of electric charges in motion.

electrolysis Conduction of electricity between two **electrodes**, through a solution of a substance (or a substance in its molten state) containing **ions** and accompanied by chemical changes at the electrodes. *See also* **electroplating**.

electrolysis, Faraday's law of Mass of a given element liberated during **electrolysis** is directly proportional to the amount of electricity consumed. When the same quantity of electricity is passed through different electrolytes, the masses of different substances liberated are directly proportional to the relative atomic weights of the substances divided by their ionic charges.

electrolyte Substance that in its molten state or in solution can conduct an electric current.

electrolytic capacitor Electrolytic cell in which a thin film of nonconducting substance has been deposited on one of the electrodes by an electric current.

electrolytic cell Apparatus that consists of **electrodes** immersed in an **electrolyte**.

electrolytic dissociation Partial or complete reversible decomposition of a substance in solution or the molten state into electrically charged **ions**.

electrolytic rectifier Rectifier that consists of two **electrodes** and an **electrolyte**, in which the current flows in one direction only.

electromagnet Temporary magnet consisting of a current-carrying coil of wire wound on a ferromagnetic core. It is the basis of many items of electrical equipment, *e.g.*, electric bells and lifting magnets.

electromagnetic induction Electromotive force (e.m.f.) produced in a conductor when it is moved in a **magnetic field.** It is the working principle of an electrical generator (*e.g.*, **dynamo**). It can give rise to a **back e.m.f.** and **eddy currents**.

electromagnetic interaction Interaction between electrically charged **elementary particles**.

electromagnetic radiation Energy that results from moving electric charges and travels in association with electric and magnetic fields, *e.g.*, radio waves, heat rays, light and X-rays, which form part of the **electromagnetic spectrum**.

electromagnetic spectrum Range of frequencies over which **electromagnetic radiations** are propagated. In order of increasing frequency (decreasing wavelength) it consists of radio waves, microwaves, infrared radiation, visible light, ultraviolet radiation, X-rays and gamma rays.

electromagnetic units [EMU] System of electrical units based on a unit magnetic pole.

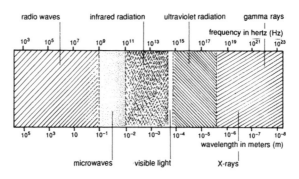

Electromagnetic spectrum

electromagnetic wave Wave formed by electric and magnetic fields, *i.e.*, of **electromagnetic radiation.** Such waves do not require a medium in which to propagate and will travel in a vacuum.

electromagnetism Combination of an **electric field** and a **magnetic field,** their interaction with stationary or moving **electric charges,** and their study and application. It therefore applies to light and other forms of **electromagnetic radiation,** as well as to devices such as electromagnets, electric motors and generators.

electromotive force (e.m.f.) Potential difference of a source of electric current, such as an **electrolytic cell** (battery) or generator. Often it can be measured only at equilibrium (when there is no current flow). Alternative name: voltage.

electron Fundamental negatively charged subatomic particle (radius 2.81777×10^{-15} m; rest mass 9.109558×10^{-31}; charge 1.602192×10^{-19}). Every neutral atom has as many orbiting electrons as there are **protons** in its **nucleus.** A flow of electrons constitutes an electric current.

electron affinity Energy liberated when an **electron** is acquired by a neutral atom.

electron capture 1. Formation of a negative ion through the capture of an **electron** by a substance. 2. Transformation of a **proton** into a **neutron** in the nucleus of an atom (accompanied by the emission of X-rays) through the capture of an orbital electron, so converting the element into another with an atomic number one less.

electron charge (*e*) Charge on an electron, a fundamental physical constant equal to 1.602102×10^{-19} coulombs.

electron configuration *See* **configuration.**

electron density Density of **electric charge.**

electron diffraction Method of determining the arrangement of the atoms in a solid, and hence its crystal structure, by the **diffraction** of a beam of **electrons.**

electron gun Electrode assembly for producing a narrow beam of electrons, as used, *e.g.,* in **cathode-ray tubes.**

electronics Branch of science concerned with the study of electricity in a vacuum, in gases and in **semiconductors.**

electron lens Arrangement of **electrodes** or of permanent or **electromagnets** used to focus or divert beams of electrons in the same way as an optical lens modifies a beam of light, as in *e.g.,* an **electron microscope.**

electron microscope Instrument that uses a beam of electrons from an **electron gun** to produce magnified images of extremely small objects, beyond the range of an optical microscope.

electron multiplier Alternative name for **photomultiplier.**

electron octet *See* **octet.**

electron optics Study of the control of free electrons by curved electric and magnet fields, particularly the use of such fields to focus and deflect beams of electrons.

electron probe microanalysis (EPM) Quantitative analysis of small amounts of substances by focusing a beam of electrons on to a point on the surface of the sample so that characteristics X-ray intensities are produced.

electron radius (r_e) Radius of an electron, a fundamental physical constant equal to 2.81777×10^{-15} m.

electron rest mass (m_e) Mass of an electron, a fundamental physical constant equal to 9.10908×10^{-31} kg.

electron-spin resonance (ESR) Branch of microwave spectroscopy in which radiation of measurable frequency and wavelength is used to supply energy to protons.

electron volt (eV) General unit of energy equal to work done on an electron when it passes through potential gradient of 1 volt.

electrophoresis Movement of charged **colloid** particles in a solution placed in an **electric field**.

electrophorus Device for producing charges by electrostatic induction.

electroplating Deposition of a thin coating of a metal using **electrolysis**. The object to be plated is the **cathode**, and the plating metal is the **anode**. Metal ions are stripped from the anode, pass through the electrolyte, and are deposited on the cathode.

electroscope Instrument for detecting electric charges or gaseous ions.

electrostatic field Electric field associated with stationary electric charges.

electrostatic printer Machine that prints by heat-fusing finely powdered carbon to paper on which characters have been "imprinted" as patterns of electrostatic charge. *See also* **xerography**.

electrostatics Branch of electricity concerned with the study of electrical charges at rest.

electrostatic units (ESU) System of electrical units based on the force exerted between two electric charges.

electrostriction Change in the dimensions of a **dielectric** that is caused by the reorientation of molecules when an **electric field** is applied.

element 1. Substance consisting of similar **atoms** of the same atomic number. It cannot be decomposed by chemical action to a simpler substance. Alternative name: chemical element. *See also* **isotope.** 2. In physics, one of several lenses in a compound lens, or one of several components in an electrical circuit. 3. General term for the high-resistance coil in an electric fire or heater.

elementary particle Subatomic particle not known to be made up of simpler particles.

elevation of boiling point Rise in the boiling point of a liquid caused by dissolving a substance in the liquid.

emission spectrum Spectrum obtained when the light from a luminous source undergoes dispersion and is observed directly.

emulsion Colloidal suspension of one liquid dispersed in another.

endothermic Describing a process in which heat is taken in; *e.g.*, in many chemical reaction. *See also* **exothermic.**

energy Capacity for doing work, measured in joules. Energy takes various forms; *e.g.* **kinetic energy, potential energy,** electrical energy, chemical energy, **heat, light** and **sound**. All forms of energy can be regarded as being aspects of kinetic or potential energy, *e.g.*, heat energy in a substance is the kinetic energy of that substance's molecules.

energy level The energy of **electrons** in an atom is not continuously variable, but has a discrete set of values, *i.e.*, energy levels. At any instant the energy of a given electron can correspond to only one of these levels. *See* **Bohr theory**.

engine Machine for converting one form of energy into another form, or for producing a **mechanical advantage**. In many engines, combustion of a fuel converts its chemical energy into usable mechanical energy. Alternative name: motor.

enrichment In the nuclear industry, processing an ore or fuel to increase the proportion of a required fissionable **isotype**; *e.g.*, increasing the amount of uranium-235 in uranium fuel rods for nuclear reactors.

enthalpy (*H*) Amount of heat energy a substance possesses, measurable in terms of the heat change (ΔH) that accompanies a chemical reaction carried out at constant pressure. In any system, $H = U + pV$, where U is the internal energy, p the pressure and V the volume.

entropy (S) In **thermodynamics**, quantity that is a measure of a system's disorder, or the unavailability of its energy to do work. In a reversible process the change in entrophy is equal to the amount of energy adsorbed divided by the absolute temperature at which it is taken up.

epithermal neutron Neutron that has energy of between 10^{-2} and 10^2 electron volts (eV); a neutron having energy greater than that associated with thermal agitation.

equation of motion Five parameters can describe the motion of an object moving in a straight line: initial velocity (v_1), final velocity (v_2), acceleration (a), distance traveled (s) and time taken (t). These give rise to five equations, each containing only four of the parameters;

$$s = \tfrac{1}{2}\, t(v_1 + v_2)$$

$$s = v_1 t + \tfrac{1}{2}\, at^2$$

$$s = v_2 t - \tfrac{1}{2}\, at^2$$

$$v_2 = v_1 + at$$

$$v_2{}^2 = v_1{}^2 + 2as$$

equation of state Any formula that connects the volume, pressure and temperature of a given system, *e.g.*, **van der Waals' equation**.

equation of time Difference between apparent time (time given by a clock) and mean solar time (sundial time).

equilibrium

equilibrium 1. An object is in **equilibrium** when the forces acting on it are such that there is no tendency for the object to move. 2. State in which no change occurs in a system if no change occurs in the surrounding environment (*e.g.*, chemical equilibrium).

erase head Part of tape recorder, video recorder or computer input/output device that erases recorded signals (data), on tape or disk, before the **write head** records new ones.

erg **Energy** transferred when a force of **1 dyne** moves through 1 cm, equivalent to 10^{-7} joules.

escape velocity Velocity that an object at a given point requires to escape from a particular **gravitational field;** *e.g.*, a rocket leaving Earth's gravity needs an escape velocity of 11,200 m s^{-1}. The velocity must be such that the **kinetic energy** of the object is greater than its **potential energy** resulting from the gravitational field. Alternative name: escape speed.

eutectic mixture Mixture of substances in such proportions that no other mixture of the same substances has a lower freezing point.

evaporation Process by which a liquid changes to its vapor. It can occur (slowly) at a temperature below the boiling point, but is faster if the liquid is heated and fastest when the liquid is boiling.

excess electron Electron that is added to a **semiconductor** from a **donor** impurity. *See also* **doping**.

excitation Addition of energy to a system, such as an atom or nucleus, causing it to transfer from its **ground state** to one of higher energy.

excitation energy Energy required for **excitation**.

excited state Energy state of an atom or molecule that is higher than the **ground state**, resulting from **excitation**. *See also* **energy level**.

{}

exclusion principle Alternative name for the **Pauli exclusion principle**.

exothermic Describing a process in which heat is evolved.

expansion of gas Increase in volume of an ideal gas is at the rate of $^1/_{273}$ of its volume at 0°C for each degree rise in temperature. *See* **Charles' Law**.

expansivity Increase in size of a substance per unit temperature rise. Linear expansivity relates to increase in length of a solid, superficial expansivity to increase in area of a solid, and volume expansivity to increase in volume of a solid, liquid or gas (*see* **expansion of gas**). Alternative name: thermal expansion.

extrinsic semiconductor Semiconductor that has its conductivity increased by the introduction of tiny, but controlled, amounts of certain impurities. *See* **doping**.

eye Sense organ for detecting light. Light passes through the transparent cornea and lens, which together focus it on the light-sensitive retina at the back of the eye. The amount of light entering is controlled by the pupil, whose size can be changed by the iris. Ciliary muscles stretch the lens to change its shape for focusing on near or far objects. A liquid (aqueous humor) between the cornea and the lens, and a jelly-like fluid (vitreous humor) between the lens and the retina keep the eyeball in shape.

F

face-centered cube Crystal structure that is cubic with an **atom** or **ion** at the center of each of the six faces of the cube in addition to the eight at its corners.

Fahrenheit scale Temperature scale on which the freezing point of water is 32°F and the boiling point 212°F. It was named after the German physicist Gabriel Fahrenheit (1686–1736).

fall-out Radioactive substances that fall to Earth from the atmosphere after a nuclear explosion.

farad (F) Unit of electrical **capacitance**, defined as the capacitance that, when charged by a potential difference of 1 volt, carries a charge of 1 coulomb.

faraday (F) Unit of electric charge equal to the quantity of charge that during **electrolysis** liberates one gram equivalent of an element. It has the value 9.65×10^4 coulombs per gram-equivalent. It was named after the British scientist Michael Faraday (1791–1867). *See also* **farad**.

Faraday cage Shield, commonly made of metal wire, used to protect apparatus or equipment from external electric fields.

Faraday constant (*F*) Fundamental physical constant, the electric charge carried by one mole of singly charged ions or electrons, equal to 9.6487×10^4 coulombs per mole. It is the product of the **Avogadro constant** and the **electron charge**.

Faraday effect Rotation of the plane of vibration of a beam of polarized light passing through a substance such as glass, in the direction of an applied magnetic field.

Faraday's laws of electrolysis 1. The amount of chemical decomposition that takes place during **electrolysis** is proportional to the electric current passed. 2. The amounts of substances liberated during electrolysis are proportional to their chemical equivalent weights.

Faraday's laws of electromagnetic induction 1. An induced **electromotive force** is established in an electric circuit whenever the magnetic field linking that circuit changes. 2. The magnitude of the induced electromotive force in any circuit is proportional to the rate of change of the **magnetic flux** linking the circuit.

farsightedness Visual defect in which the eyeball is too short (front to back) so that light rays entering the **eye** from near objects would be brought to a focus at a point behind the retina. It can be corrected by spectacles or contact lenses made from converging (convex) lenses. Alternative name: hypermetropia.

fast neutron Neutron produced by **nuclear fission** that has lost little of its energy and travels too fast to produce further fission and sustain a **chain reaction** (unlike a slow, or thermal, neutron).

fatigue In physics, permanent weakness in a substance that results from stresses placed upon it.

feedback Process in which a system or device is controlled or modified as a result of its activity. In positive feedback, the activity is increased; in negative feedback, it is decreased.

ferrimagnetism Property of certain compounds in which the **magnetic moments** of neighboring ions align in antiparallel fashion (*e.g.*, **ferrites**).

ferrite Nonconducting ceramic material that exhibits **ferrimagnetism** used to make powerful magnets for radars and other high-frequency electronic apparatus, such as computer memories.

ferromagnetism Property of certain substances that in a
magnetizing field have induced magnetism (because of aligned
magnetic moments), which persists when the field is removed
and they become permanent magnets. The magnetized regions
are called **magnetic domains**. Examples of ferromagnetic
materials include iron, cobalt and their alloys.

fiber optics Branch of optics that uses bundles of pure glass fibers
within straight or curved "pipes," along which light travels as it
is internally reflected. A modulated light signal can carry much
more data (*e.g.*, computer data, telephone signals, television
channels) than a wire of similar dimensions.

field 1. In physics, region in which one object exerts a force on
another object; *e.g.*, **electric field, gravitational field,
magnetic field**. 2. In optics, area that is visible through an
optical instrument. 3. In computing, specific part of a **record**, or
a group of characters that make up one piece of information.

field coil Coil used for producing a **magnetic field** in an
electromagnet or other electric machine.

field-effect transistor (FET) Type of transistor that consists of a
conducting channel formed from a wafer of **semiconductor**
material, the resistance of which is controlled by the voltage
applied to one or more input **gates**.

field emission microscope Microscope used for the observation
of the position of atoms in a surface.

field magnet Permanent **magnet** or **electromagnet,** the purpose
of which is to provide a **magnetic field** in an electric machine.

filament Fine wire of high **resistance** that is heated by passing an
electric current directly through it. Filaments are used in electric
fires and incandescent lamps.

film 1. Thin layer of one substance on the surface of another
substance, *e.g.*, oil floating on water. Thin films can sometimes
diffract light and produce rainbow colors (*see* **diffraction**).

2. Plastic strip carrying a light-sensitive emulsion that is used in photography.

filter 1. In optics, light-absorbing semitransparent material that passes only certain wavelengths (colors). 2. In electronics, device that passes only certain a.c. frequencies.

filter pump Simple vacuum pump in which a jet of water draws air molecules from the system. It can produce only low pressures and is commonly used to increase the speed of filtration by drawing through the filtrate.

fine structure Splitting of certain lines in a **line spectrum** into a number of further discrete lines, which are observable only when high resolution is employed.

fission Splitting. In atomic physics, disintegration of an atom into parts with similar masses, usually with the release of energy and one or more neutrons (*see* **nuclear fission**).

fission product Isotope produced by **nuclear fission**, with a mass equal to roughly half that of the fissile material.

fission spectrum Energy distribution of **neutrons** released during **nuclear fission**.

fixed point Standard temperature chosen to define a **temperature scale** or at which properties are measured, *e.g.*, the **ice point** (0°C) and the **steam point** (100°C). Alternative name; fixed temperature.

flash point Lowest temperature at which a substance or a mixture gives off sufficient vapor to produce a flash on the application of a flame.

F-layer Alternative name for the **Appleton layer** of the **ionosphere**.

Fleming's rules *See* **left-hand rule; right-hand rule**.

flip-flop Electronic component or circuit that can be switched
from one of its two stable states to the other by an electric
pulse; a bistable device. Flip-flops are frequently used in
computers.

floppy disk Flexible, portable magnetic disk that provides data
and program storage for **microcomputers**. The disk may be
enclosed in a flexible or a rigid casing. Alternative name:
diskette. *See also* **hard disk**.

flotation, principle of A floating object displaces its own weight
of fluid (liquid or gas). An object floats if its weight equals the
upthrust on it. *See also* **Archimedes' principle**.

fluid Form of matter that can flow; thus both gases and liquids are
fluids. Fluids can offer no permanent resistance to changes of
shape. Resistance to flow is manifest as **viscosity**.

fluidics Study and use of fluid flow to control instruments or
industrial processes.

fluidity Property of flowing easily; the opposite of **viscosity**.

fluidization Technique whereby a finely divided solid acquires
characteristics of fluid by upward passage of a gas through it.

fluorescence Emission of radiation (generally visible light) after
absorption of radiation of another wavelength (usually
ultraviolet or near-ultraviolet) or electrons; unlike
phosphorescence, it ceases when the stimulating source is
removed. *See also* **luminescence.**

fluorescent lamp Mercury-vapor discharge lamp that uses
phosphors to produce light by **fluorescence**.

flux Rate of flow of mass, volume or energy per unit area normal
to the direction of flow.

flux density Magnetic flux or luminous flux per unit of cross-
sectional area.

fluxmeter Instrument for measuring **magnetic flux**.

FM Abbreviation of **frequency modulation.**

f-**number** Method of denoting the diameter of a lens aperture in a camera; for a simple lens it is the **focal length** divided by the diameter of the aperture. The smaller the *f*-number, the larger the aperture. In the usual sequence *f*22, *f*11, *f*8, *f*5.6, *f*4, etc., each aperture has twice the area (and hence admits twice the amount of light) as the preceding one in the series.

focal length Distance from the center of a lens or mirror to its **focal point**. Alternative name: focal distance.

focal point In optics, the point at which light rays meet after refraction or reflection.

force (*F*) Influence that can make a stationary object move, or a moving object change speed or direction, *i.e.*, that changes the object's momentum. For a body of mass *m* and acceleration *a*, the force $F = ma$. Its SI unit is the **newton.**

force meter Instrument resembling a spring balance used for measuring force. *See also* **newton meter.**

force ratio Alternative name for **mechanical advantage.**

Fortin barometer Mercury **barometer,** used for the accurate measurement of atmospheric pressure. It was named after the French physicist Jean Fortin (1750–1831).

FORTRAN Acronym of FORmula TRANslation, a high-level computer programming language designed for mathematical and scientific use.

fossil fuel Mineral fuel that is formed from the remains of living organisms; *e.g.*, coal, natural gas, petroleum.

Foucault pendulum Long pendulum with a heavy bob whose plane of swing appears to turn slowly because of Earth's rotation. It was named after the French physicist Jean Foucault (1819–1868).

f.p.s. units System of units based on the foot, pound and second.

frame of reference Set of points, lines or planes for defining positions.

free electron Electron free to move from one atom or molecule to another under the influence of an **electric current**.

free energy Measure of the ability of a system to perform work. *See also* **Gibbs free energy** (Gibbs function).

free fall Movement of an object in a gravitational field, with no other forces acting on it (when it will appear to be weightless). At a particular place all objects falling freely under gravity (in a vacuum or when air resistance is negligible) have the same constant acceleration irrespective of their masses. On Earth this is g, the **acceleration of free fall** (9.80665 ms^{-2}).

freezing Solidification of a liquid that occurs when it is cooled sufficiently (to below its freezing point).

freezing mixture Mixture of two substances (*e.g.*, ice and salt) that absorbs heat and can be used to produce a temperature of below 0°C. *See also* **eutectic mixture**.

freezing point Temperature at which a liquid solidifies. Alternative name: solidification point.

Frenkel defect Crystal disorder that occurs when an ion occupies a vacant interstitial site, leaving its proper site empty.

frequency (*f*) Rate of recurrence of wave, *i.e.*, number of cycles, oscillations or vibrations in unit time, usually one second. The frequency of a wave is inversely proportional to the **wavelength** λ; *i.e.*, $f = c/\lambda$, where c is the velocity of the wave. The SI unit of frequency is the **hertz** (which corresponds to 1 cycle per second).

frequency modulation (FM) Method of radio transmission, used in the short wavelengths, in which the information content is conveyed by means of variations in the **frequency** of the **carrier wave**.

Fresnel lens Lens that is formed by cutting a series of stepped concentric circles. It is flatter and lighter than a conventional lens of equivalent power, but the optical quality is not high. It was named after the French physicist Augustin Fresnel (1788–1827).

friction Resistance offered to sliding or rolling of one surface on another. It is a **force**, a type of **adhesion**.

fuel cell Device that uses the oxidation of a liquid or gaseous fuel to produce electricity. Thus the chemical energy of the fuel is converted directly to electrical energy, without the intermediate stages of a heat engine and a generator. *E.g.*, hydrogen and oxygen flowing over porous platinum electrodes immersed in hot potassium hydroxide solution react to produce water and generate a voltage across the electrodes.

fundamental units Units of length, mass and time that form the basis of most systems of units.

fuse Device used for protecting against an excess **electric current** passing through a circuit. It consists of a piece of metal, connected into the circuit, that heats and melts (thereby breaking the circuit) when the current exceeds a certain value.

fusion Act of melting or joining together. *See also* **nuclear fusion**.

fusion reaction *See* **nuclear fusion**; **thermonuclear reaction**.

fusion reactor *See* **nuclear reactor**.

G

gain Increase in power produced by an **amplifier**, the ratio of the amplitude of the output to that of the input.

Galilean telescope Optical refracting telescope that uses a converging (convex) lens as its objective and a diverging (concave) lens as its eyepiece. It produces an upright image, and is the arrangement used, *e.g.*, in opera glasses. It was named after the Italian astronomer and physicist Galileo Galilei (1564–1642).

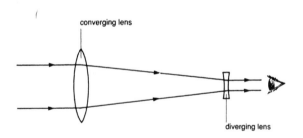

converging lens

diverging lens

Galilean telescope is used in opera glasses

galvanic cell Alternative name for a **voltaic cell**.

galvanometer Device that detects or measures small electric currents passing through it.

gamma radiation Penetrating form of **electromagnetic radiation** of shorter wavelength than **X-rays**, produced, *e.g.*, during the decay of certain **radio-isotopes**.

gamma rays High-energy **photons** that make up **gamma radiation**.

gas Form (phase) of matter in which the atoms and molecules move randomly with high speeds, occupy all the space available, and are comparatively far apart; a vapor. A liquid heated above its boiling point changes into a gas.

gas constant (R) Constant in the **gas equation**, value 8.31 J mol^{-1} K^{-1}. Alternative name: universal molar gas constant.

gas-cooled reactor Nuclear reactor in which the cooling (heat-exchanging) medium is a gas, usually carbon dioxide.

gas equation For n moles of a gas, $pV = nRT$, where p = pressure, V = volume, n = number of moles, R = the **gas constant** and T = absolute temperature.

gas laws Relationships between pressure, volume and temperature of a gas. The combination of **Boyle's**, **Charles'** and **Gay-Lussac's laws** is the **gas equation**.

gas thermometer Thermometer based on the variation in pressure or volume of a gas. Alternative name: constant-volume gas thermometer.

gas turbine Form of internal combustion engine in which the expansion of the hot gases resulting from the combustion of the fuel is used to drive a turbine (coupled to the compressor). Alternative name: jet engine.

gate In computing, an electronic circuit (switch) that produces a single output signal from two or more input signals. Alternative name: logic element.

gauss (G) Unit of magnetic flux density equal to 10^{-4} **tesla**, by which the gauss has been replaced in the SI system.

Gay-Lussac's law of volume When gases react their volumes are in a simple ratio to each other and to the volume of products, at the same temperature and pressure. It was named after the French chemist and physicist Joseph Gay-Lussac (1778–1850).

gear Toothed wheel that engages with another toothed wheel to transfer rotation from one shaft to another. If the two gears have different numbers of teeth (the ratio of these numbers is the gear ratio), the second shaft rotates at a different speed from the drive shaft.

Geiger counter Instrument for detecting atomic and subatomic particles (*e.g.*, **alpha** and **beta particles**), used for radioactivity measurements. It was named after the German physicist Hans Geiger (1882–1945). Alternative name: Geiger-Müller counter. *See also* **counter**.

Geiger-Nuttal law Empirical law for calculating the distance that an **alpha particle** can travel once it is emitted from a radioactive substance.

Geissler tube Electric discharge tube, containing traces of gas at very low pressure, that glows when a high-voltage current flows between metal electrodes sealed into it. It was named after the German apparatus-maker Heinrich Geissler (1814–1879).

gel Jelly-like colloidal solution. *See* **colloid**.

general theory of relativity Part of the theory of **relativity** (along with the special theory).

generator Machine for converting mechanical energy into electrical energy. Alternative name: electric generator. *See also* **alternator; dynamo**.

geodesic Describing structures, *e.g.*, domes, that are made from large numbers of identical components, and that have the load distributed evenly throughout the structure.

geomagnetism Earth's magnetic field.

geophysics Study of the physics of Earth.

geostationary orbit Path of an artificial Earth satellite at such a height (35,900 km) that it takes 24 hours to make one complete **orbit**, during which time Earth makes one revolution on its axis and so the satellite remains above the same place on Earth's surface. It is used mainly for communications satellites. Alternative names: stationary orbit, synchronous orbit.

GeV Abbreviation of giga-electron volt, which is 10^9 electron volts.

Gibbs free energy (G) Measure of the energy that would be liberated or absorbed during a reversible process. $G = H - TS$, where H is heat content, T thermodynamic temperature and S **entropy.** Alternative name: Gibbs function. It was named after the American chemist and physicist Josiah Gibbs (1839–1903).

glass electrode Glass membrane electrode used to measure hydrogen ion concentration or pH.

glove box Closed box that has gloves fixed into holes in the walls, and in which operations involving hazardous substances, such as radioactive materials or toxic chemicals, may be carried out safely. Alternative name: dry box.

gluon Subatomic particle of the type believed to hold **quarks** together.

gold-leaf electroscope Type of **electroscope** that has two pieces of gold foil (gold leaf) at the end of a metal rod inside a glass jar. If an electrostatic charge is brought up to the rod, the gold leaves move apart.

gradient Rate of rise or fall of a variable quantity such as temperature or pressure.

Graham's law Velocity of diffusion of a gas is inversely proportional to the square root of its density. It was named after the British chemist Thomas Graham (1805–1869).

gram Unit of mass in the metric system. Alternative name: gramme.

gram molecule Molecular weight of a substance in grams; 1 mole.

gravimeter Instrument that measures variations in Earth's gravitational field by detecting changes in the force (of gravity) acting on a suspended weight. It is used in prospecting for deposits of minerals (including petroleum), which affect the gravitational field near them.

gravitation, law of Alternative name for **Newton's law of gravitation**.

gravitational constant (G) Constant in **Newton's law of gravitation**. Alternative name: universal gravitational constant.

gravitational field Region in which an object with mass exerts a force of attraction on another such object because of **gravity**.

graviton Hypothetical particle that is believed to cause the gravitational effect between subatomic particles.

gravity Force of attraction that one object has on another because of their masses. The strength of the force is described by **Newton's law of gravitation**. The term is often used to refer to the force of gravity of Earth.

gray (Gy) Amount of absorbed radiation dose in SI units, equal to supplying 1 joule of energy per kg. It is equivalent to 100 rad (the unit it superseded).

grid 1. In electricity, network of wires and cables that distribute electricity from power stations to where it is used. 2. In electronics, an electrode (other than the anode and cathode) that controls the flow of current through a **thermionic valve** (*e.g.*, triode, tetrode).

ground state Lowest energy state of an atom or molecule, from which it can be raised to a higher energy state by **excitation**. *See also* **energy level**.

gyromagnetic ratio Ratio of the **magnetic moment** of an atom or nucleus to its **angular momentum**.

gyroscope Device in which a flywheel rotates at a high speed and because of this resists any change in direction of its axis of rotation. Gyroscopes are used in stabilizers for ships and guns and in guidance systems.

H

hadron Any **elementary particle** that interacts strongly with other particles, including **baryons** and **mesons**.

half-cell Half of an **electrolytic cell**, consisting of an electrode immersed in an **electrolyte**.

half-life 1. Time taken for something whose decay is exponential to reduce to half its value. 2. More specifically, time taken for half the nuclei of a **radioactive** substance to decay spontaneously. The half-life of some unstable substances is only a few seconds or less, whereas for other substances it may be thousands of years; *e.g.*, lawrencium has a half-life of 8 seconds, and the **isotope** plutonium-239 has a half-life of 24,400 years.

halo White or rainbow-colored ring sometimes observed around the sun or moon, caused by light **refraction** through minute ice crystals in Earth's atmosphere.

hard copy In computing, document that people can read (*e.g.*, a printout in plain language).

hard disk Rigid magnetic disk that provides data and program storage for computers, including microcomputers. Hard disks can hold a high density of data. When used in a microcomputer, they are usually not portable. Alternative name: diskette. *See also* **floppy disk; winchester**.

hardware Electronic, electrical, magnetic, and mechanical parts that make up a **computer** system. *See also* **software**.

harmonic Frequency of a wave, *e.g.*, a sound wave, that is a whole-number multiple of the frequency of another wave (known as the fundamental). Alternative name: overtone.

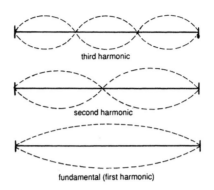

Fundamental and first two harmonics

harmonic motion Alternative name for **simple harmonic motion**.

harmonic series Series of *e.g.*, sounds in which each is a **harmonic** of a fundamental sound.

head In a tape recorder, video recorder, record player or computer input/output device, an electromagnetic component that can read, erase or write signals off or onto tapes and disks.

heat Form of **energy**, the energy of motion (kinetic energy) possessed by the atoms or molecules of all substances at temperatures above **absolute zero**.

heat balance Statement of all sources of heat and all of its uses for an industrial process or piece of equipment.

heat capacity Quantity of heat required to produce unit rise of temperature in an object. *See also* **specific heat capacity**.

heat engine Machine that converts heat into mechanical energy (for doing useful work).

heat exchanger Device that employs two separate streams of fluid (gas or liquid) for heating or cooling one of them; *e.g.*, a car radiator uses air flow to cool water.

Heaviside layer Region of the **ionosphere** at an altitude of 110–120 km. It is the most regular of the ionized layers that reflect radio waves, and has its greater effect during the hours of daylight. It was named after the British scientist Oliver Heaviside (1850–1935). Alternative name: E-layer. *See also* **F-layer.**

hecto- Metric prefix for a multiple of 10^2; denotes 100 times.

Heisenberg uncertainty principle The precise position and momentum of an electron cannot be determined simultaneously. It was named after the German physicist Werner Heisenberg (1901–1976).

Helmholtz free energy (*F*) Thermodynamic quantity equal to $U - TS$, where U is the **internal energy**, T the thermodynamic temperature and S the **entropy.** It was named after the German physicist Hermann Helmholtz (1821–1894).

henry (H) Unit of electrical **inductance**, defined as the inductance that produces an induced electromotive force of 1 volt for a current change of 1 ampere per second. It was named after the American physicist Joseph Henry (1797–1878).

Henry's law Weight of gas dissolved by a liquid is proportional to the gas pressure.

hertz (Hz) Unit of frequency in the SI system. 1 Hz = 1 cycle per second. It was named after the German physicist Heinrich Hertz (1858–1894).

Hess's law Total energy change resulting from a chemical reaction is dependent only on the initial and final states, and is independent of the reaction route. It was named after the Austrian physicist Victor Hess (1883–1964).

hetero- Prefix denoting other or different. *See also* **homo-.**

heterogeneous Relating to more than one **phase** (*e.g.*, describing a chemical reaction that involves one or more **solids**, in addition to a **gas** or a **liquid** phase); describing a system of nonuniform composition. *See also* **homogeneous.**

high frequency (HF) 1. Radio frequency between 30,000 and 3,000 KHz, used in radio communications. 2. Rapidly alternating electric current or wave.

high-vacuum distillation Alternative name for **molecular distillation**.

holography Method of reproducing a three-dimensional image that employs **interference** and **diffraction** of **laser** light to store and subsequently release light waves.

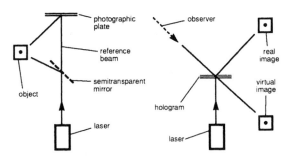

Principle of holography

homo- Prefix denoting the same or similar. *See also* **hetero-.**

homogeneous Relating to a single **phase** (*e.g.*, describing a chemical reaction in which all the reactants are solids, or liquids or gases); describing a system of uniform composition.

Hooke's law For a material being stretched within its **elastic limit,** the extension is proportional to the force producing it. It was named after the British scientist Robert Hooke (1635–1703).

horsepower (hp) Power needed to lift 33,000 pounds one foot in one minute. 1 horsepower = 745.7 watts.

humidity Measure of the amount of water vapor in a gas, *e.g.*, the air, usually expressed as a percentage. Relative humidity is the amount of vapor divided by the maximum amount of vapor the gas will hold (at a particular temperature).

hydraulics Branch of engineering concerned with the flow of liquids in pipes and channels, the pumping of liquids, and their use for the transmission and generation of power.

hydrogen bomb Powerful explosive device that uses the sudden release of energy from **nuclear fusion** (of **deuterium** and **tritium** atoms). Alternative name: thermonuclear bomb.

hydrogen electrode Half-cell that consists of hydrogen gas bubbling around a platinum electrode, covered in platinum black (very finely divided platinum). It is immersed in a molar acid solution and used for determining standard **electrode potentials.** Alternative name: hydrogen half-cell.

hydrogen half-cell Alternative name for **hydrogen electrode.**

hydrogen ion H + Positively charged hydrogen atom; a **proton.** A characteristic of an acid is the production of hydrogen ions, which in aqueous solution are hydrated to hydroxonium ions, H_3O^+.

hydrogen spectrum Spectrum produced when an electric discharge is passed through hydrogen gas. The hydrogen molecules dissociate and the atoms emit light at a series of characteristic frequencies. *See also* **Balmer series**.

hydrometer Instrument for measuring the density of a liquid. It consists of a weighted glass bulb with a long graduated stem, which floats in the liquid being tested.

hydrosol Aqueous solution of a **colloid.**

hydrostatics Branch of science that deals with fluids at rest.

hygrometer Instrument for measuring the **humidity** of air, the amount of water vapor in the atmosphere.

hyperfine structure Fine structure that is observed only when very high resolution is employed.

hypermetropia Alternative name for **farsightedness**.

hyperon Member of a group of short-lived **elementary particles** that are greater in mass than the **neutron**.

hypotonic Having a lower than normal **osmotic pressure**.

hysteresis In physics, the lag or delay between a cause and its effect, as in the magnetization of a magnetic substance.

I

ice point Freezing point of water, 0°C, used as a fixed point on temperature scales.

ideal crystal Crystal structure that is considered as perfect, containing no defects.

ideal gas Hypothetical gas with molecules of negligible size that experience no intermolecular forces. Such a gas would in theory obey the **gas laws** exactly. Alternative name: perfect gas.

ideal solution Hypothetical solution that obeys **Raoult's law** exactly.

illumination *(E)* Brightness of light on a surface, given as the intensity per unit area, expressed in lux (lumens per square meter). Alternative name: illuminance.

image In optics, point from which rays of light entering the **eye** appear to have originated. A real image, *e.g.*, one formed by a converging lens, can be focused on a screen; a virtual image, *e.g.*, one formed in a plane mirror, can be seen only by the eyes of the observer.

image converter Electron tube for converting infrared or other invisible images into visible images.

impedance *(Z)* Property of an electric circuit or circuit component that opposes the passage of current. For **direct current** (d.c.) it is equal to the **resistance** *(R)*. For **alternating current** (a.c.) the **reactance** *(X)* also has an effect, such that $Z^2 = R^2 + X^2$, or $Z = R + iX$, where $i^2 = -1$.

imperial system Comprehensive system of weights and measures (feet and inches, **avoirdupois** weights, prints and gallons, etc.)

that was formerly used throughout the British Empire. Many units are still in widespread use in Britain, but **SI units** have replaced the imperial system for scientific measurement.

implosion Opposite of explosion; an inward burst, *e.g.*, as when a vacuum-filled vessel crumples in air.

impulse In physics, when two objects collide, over the period of impact there is a large reactionary force between them whose time integral is the impulse of the force (equal to either object's change of momentum).

incandescence Light emission that results from the high temperature of a substance; *e.g.*, the filament in an electric lamp is incandescent. *See also* **luminescence**.

induced magnetism Creation of a magnet by aligning the magnetic **domains** in a ferromagnetic substance by placing it in the **magnetic field** of a permanent magnet or electromagnet.

induced radioactivity Alternative name for **artificial radioactivity**.

inductance 1. Property of a current-carrying electric circuit or circuit component that causes it to form a magnetic field and store magnetic energy. 2. Measurement of electromagnetic **induction**.

induction Magnetization or electrification produced in an object. 1. Electromagnetic induction is the production of an electric current in a conductor by means of a varying magnetic field near it. 2. Magnetic induction is the production of a magnetic field in an unmagnetized metal by a nearby magnetic field. 3. Electrostatic induction is the production of an electric charge on an object by a charged object brought near it.

induction coil Type of **transformer** for producing high-voltage alternating current from a low-voltage source. Induction coils can be used to produce a high-voltage pulse, *e.g.*, for firing spark plugs in a gasoline engine.

induction heating Heating effect that arises from the electric current induced in a conducting material by an alternating **magnetic field**.

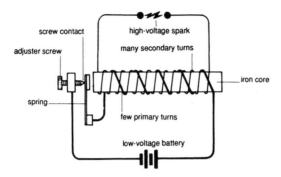

Simple induction coil

induction motor Electric motor that consists of two coils, one stationary (the stator) and one moving (the rotor). An electric current is fed to the stator, which creates a magnetic field and induces currents in the rotor. The interaction between the magnetic field and the induced currents causes the rotor to turn.

inductor Any component of an electrical circuit that possesses significant **inductance.** Alternative name: choke, coil.

inertia Resistance offered by an object to a change in its state of rest or motion. Inertia is a property of the **mass** of an object.

infrared radiation Electromagnetic radiation in the wavelength range from 0.75 μm to 1 mm approximately; between the visible and microwave regions of the **electromagnetic spectrum.** It is emitted by all objects at temperatures above absolute zero, as heat (thermal) radiation.

infrasound Sound wave with a frequency below the threshold of human hearing, *i.e.,* less than about 20 Hz.

input device Part of a **computer** that feeds in with **data** and **program** instructions. The many types of input devices include a keyboard, punched card reader, paper tape reader, optical character recognition, light pen (with a VDU) and various types of devices equipped with a **read head** to input magnetically recorded data (*e.g.* on magnetic disk, tape or drum).

insulation

insulation Layer of material (an **insulator**) used to prevent the flow of **electricity** or **heat**.

insulator Substance that is a poor conductor of **electricity** or **heat**; a nonconductor. Most nonmetallic elements (except carbon) and polymers are good insulators.

integrated circuit Very small solid-state circuit consisting of interconnected **semiconductor** devices such as diodes, transistors, capacitors and resistors printed into a single silicon chip.

intensity Power of sound, light or other wave-form (*e.g.*, the loudness of a sound or the brightness of light), determined by the **amplitude** of the wave.

interaction In atomic physics, exchange of energy between a particle and a second one or an **electromagnetic wave**.

interface Boundary of contact (the common surface) of two adjacent **phases**, either or both of which may be solid, liquid or gaseous.

interference Interaction between two or more waves of the same frequency emitted from coherent sources. The waves may reinforce each other or tend to cancel each other; the resultant wave is the algebraic sum of the component waves. The phenomenon occurs with **electromagnetic waves** and **sound**.

intermediate frequency Frequency to which radio signal is converted during heterodyne reception (which involves the superimposition of two radio waves of different frequencies).

intermediate neutron Neutron that has energy between that of a **fast neutron** and a **thermal neutron**.

intermolecular force Force that binds one molecule to another. Intermolecular forces are much weaker than the bonding forces holding together the atoms of a molecule. *See also* **van der Waals' force**.

internal combustion engine Engine that produces power through the combustion of a fuel/air mixture inside an enclosed space (in gasoline and diesel engines, a cylinder fitted with a piston).

internal conversion Effect on the nucleus of an atom produced by a gamma ray **photon** emerging from it and giving up its energy on meeting an electron of the same atom.

internal energy Total quantity of energy in a substance, the sum of its **kinetic energy** and **potential energy**.

internal friction *See* **viscosity**.

internal resistance Electrical **resistance** in a circuit of the source of current, *e.g.*, a cell.

international candle Former unit of **luminous intensity**.

interstitial atom Atom that is in a position other than a normal **lattice** place.

inverse square law Law that quantifies the falling off of an effect (*e.g.*, electrostatic, gravitational and magnetic fields, light radiation) with the square of the distance to the source. For instance in optics, the quantity of light from a given source on a surface of definite area is inversely proportional to the square of the distance between the source and the surface.

ion Atom or molecule that has positive or negative electric charge because of the loss or gain of one or more electrons. Many inorganic compounds dissociate into ions when they dissolve in water. Ions are the electric current-carriers in **electrolysis** and in **discharge tubes**.

ion engine Theoretical motor for propulsion in outer space that would use a high-velocity "jet" of **ions** or **electrons**, accelerated by an electromagnetic field. Such an engine would provide drive in much the same way as the exhaust in a conventional rocket.

ionic crystal Crystal composed of **ions**. Alternative names: electrovalent crystal, polar crystal.

ionic radius Radius of an **ion** in a crystal.

ionization Formation of **ions.** It is generally achieved by chemical or electrical processes, or by dissociation of ionic compounds in

81

solution, although at extremely high temperatures (such as those in stars) heat can cause ionization.

ionization chamber Apparatus consisting of a gas-filled container with a pair of high-voltage electrodes. It is used to study the **ionization** of gases or ionizing radiation.

ionization potential Electron bonding energy, the energy required to remove an **electron** from a neutral atom.

ionizing radiation Any **radiation** that causes **ionization** by producing **ion pairs** in the medium it passes through.

ionosphere Layer of Earth's upper atmosphere that is characterized by the presence of many **ions** and free **electrons**. It is important in radio transmission.

ion pair Two charged fragments that result from simultaneous ionization of two uncharged ones; a positive and a negative **ion.**

ion propulsion Type of rocket drive that uses charged particles (*e.g.*, lithium **ions**) accelerated by an **electrostatic field**, used in an **ion engine**. Only experimental models have as yet been built.

ion pump High-vacuum pump for removing a gas from a system by ionizing its atoms or molecules and absorbing the resulting **ions** on a surface.

irradiation 1. Radiant energy per unit of intercepting area. 2. Exposure of an object to radiant energy or **ionizing radiation.**

isobar 1. Curve that relates to qualities measured at the same pressure. 2. Line drawn on a map through places having the same atmospheric pressure at a given time. 3. One of a set of atomic nuclei having the same total of **protons** and **neutrons** (*i.e.*, the same nucleon number or **mass number**) but different numbers of protons and therefore different identities.

isothermal process Process that occurs at a constant or uniform temperature; *e.g.*, the compression of a gas under constant temperature conditions. *See also* **adiabatic process.**

isotonic Having the same **osmotic pressure** as blood, or the same as the cell sap in a particular plant.

isotope One form of an atom that has the same **atomic number** but a different **atomic mass** than other forms of that atom. This results from there being different numbers of **neutrons** in the nuclei of the atoms, *e.g.*, uranium-238 (also written as U-238 or $_{238}$U) and uranium-235 are two isotopes of uranium with atomic weights of 238 and 235 respectively. The isotopes of an atom are chemically identical, although with very light isotopes the relative difference in masses may make them react at different rates. The existence of isotopes explains why most elements have nonintegral atomic masses. A few elements have no naturally occurring isotopes, including fluorine, gold, iodine and phosphorus.

isotopic number Difference between the number of **neutrons** in an **isotope** and the number of **protons**. Alternative name: neutron excess.

isotopic weight Atomic weight of an **isotope.** Alternative name: isotopic mass.

J

jet 1. Stream of liquid or gas issuing from an orifice or nozzle, or the nozzle itself (*e.g.*, the jet of a carburettor). 2. **Gas turbine** engine, particularly one used in aircraft.

jet engine Alternative name for a **gas turbine** engine used in aircraft.

joule (J) Unit of **work** and **energy** in the SI system. 1 joule is the work done by a force of 1 **newton** moving 1 meter in the direction of the force. It was named after the British physicist James Joule (1818–1889).

Joule's law 1. **Internal energy** of a given mass of gas is dependent only on its temperature and is independent of its pressure and volume. 2. If an electric current I flows through a resistance R for a time t, the heat produced Q, in joules, is given by $Q = I^2Rt$.

Joule-Thompson effect When a gas is allowed to undergo adiabatic expansion through a porous plug, the temperature of the gas usually drops. This results from the work done in breaking the intermolecular forces in the gas, and is a deviation from **Joule's law.** The effect is important in the liquefaction of gases by cooling. Alternative name: Joule-Kelvin effect.

J-particle Alternative name for **psi particle.**

junction diode Type of **diode** consisting of a layer of n-type semiconductor and p-type semiconductor. An applied voltage flows in one direction only across the junction because of the diffusion of electrons from the n-type to the p-type.

K

Kalanite Proprietary hard electrical insulating material not affected by oils.

kelvin (K) Unit of thermodynamic temperature in the SI system, named after the British physicist Lord Kelvin (William Thomson, 1824–1907). It is equal in magnitude to a degree Celsius (centigrade). *See also* **absolute temperature**.

Kelvin effect Alternative name for the **Thomson effect**.

Kelvin temperature Scale of temperature that originates at **absolute zero,** with the **triple point** of water defined as 273.16K. The freezing point of water (on which the Celsius scale is based) is 273.16K. Alternative name: Kelvin thermodynamic scale of temperature.

Kerr cell Chamber of liquid between two crossed polaroids that darkens or lightens in an electric field (applied between two electrodes). It can be used as a shutter or to modulate a light beam. It was named after the British physicist John Kerr (1824–1907).

keV Abbreviation of kilo-electron-volt, a unit of particle energy equivalent to 10^3 **electron-volts**.

keyboard Computer **input device** that a human operator uses to type in **data** as **alphanumeric** characters. It consists of a standard qwerty keyboard, usually with additional function keys.

kilo- Metric prefix meaning a thousand times ($\times 10^3$).

kilocalorie (C) Unit of energy equal to 1,000 **calories**. Alternative name: Calorie (with a capital C).

kilogram (kg) Unit of mass in the SI system, equal to 1,000 grams. 1 kg = 2.2046 lb.

kilohertz (kHz) Unit of frequency equal to 1,000 **hertz**.

kilojoule (kJ) Unit of energy equal to 1,000 **joules**.

kilometer (km) Unit of length equal to 1,000 meters. 1 km = 0.62137 miles.

kiloton Unit for the power of a nuclear explosion or warhead, equivalent to 1,000 tons of TNT.

kilowatt-hour (kWh) Unit of electrical energy equal to a rate of consumption of 1,000 watts per hour. Alternative name: unit.

kinematics Branch of **mechanics** that is concerned with interactions between **velocities** and **accelerations** of various parts of moving systems.

kinematic viscosity υ Coefficient of **viscosity** of a fluid divided by its density.

kinetic energy Energy possessed by an object because of its motion, equal to $\frac{1}{2}\,mv^2$, where m = mass and v = velocity. The kinetic energy of the particles that make up any sample of matter (*see* **kinetic theory**) determines its **heat** energy and therefore its **temperature** (except at **absolute zero**, when both are equal to zero).

kinetic theory Theory that accounts for the properties of substances in terms of the movement of their component particles (atoms or molecules). The theory is most important in describing the behavior of gases (when it is referred to as the kinetic theory of gases). An ideal gas is assumed to be made of perfectly elastic particles that collide only occasionally with each other. Thus, *e.g.*, the pressure exerted by a gas on its container is then the result of gas particles colliding with the walls of the container.

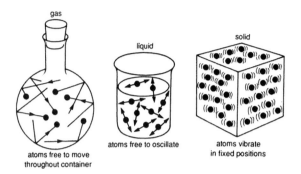

Kinetic theory describes gases, liquids and solids

Kirchhoff's law of radiation For any object, the ratio of the absorptance to the emissivity depends only on its temperature. The law was named after the German physicist Gustav Kirchhoff (1824–1887).

Kirchhoff's laws Extensions of **Ohm's law** that are used in the analysis of complex electric circuits. 1. The sum of the currents flowing at any junction is zero. 2. Around any closed path, the sum of the e.m.f.s equals the sum of the products of the currents and impedances.

L

labile Unstable; usually applied with respect to particular conditions, *e.g.*, heat-labile.

lambda particle Type of **elementary particle** with no electric charge.

lambda point Temperature at which liquid helium (helium I) becomes the **superfluid** known as helium II.

Lambert's law Equal fractions of incident light radiation are absorbed by successive layers of equal thickness of the light-absorbing substance. It was named after the German mathematician and physicist Johann Lambert (1728–1777).

lamina Thin flat sheet of a material of uniform thickness.

laminar flow Streamlined, or nonturbulent, flow in a gas or liquid.

Laplace law Alternative name for **Ampère's law**.

Larmor precession Orbital motion of an **electron** about the **nucleus** of an atom when it is subjected to a small magnetic field. The electron precesses about the direction of the magnetic field. It was named after the British physicist Joseph Larmor (1857–1942).

laser Acronym of "light amplification by stimulated emission of radiation." It is a device that produces a powerful monochromatic and coherent beam of light by stimulation of emission from excited atoms. Lasers are used in **holography**, for measuring and surveying, as industrial and medical cutting tools and for many other purposes. *See also* **maser**.

latch Electric circuit designed to stay functioning even when the original signal that triggered it is switched off (*e.g.*, in an alarm circuit or counter readout).

latent heat Heat energy that is needed to produce a change of state during the melting (solid-to-liquid change) or vaporization (liquid-to-vapor/gas change) of a substance; it causes no rise in temperature. This heat energy is released when the substance reverts to its former state (by freezing/solidifying or condensing/liquefying).

lateral inversion Apparent reversal of an image left to right when viewed in a plane mirror, resulting from the actual front-to-back reversal as required by the laws of reflection.

latitude Imaginary line drawn parallel to the equator around Earth. The equator is 0° latitude, and the distance between the equator and the poles is divided into 90° of latitude. Using latitude in combination with **longitude**, any position on Earth's surface can be denoted. Alternative name: parallel.

lattice Regular network of atoms, ions or molecules in a **crystal**.

lattice energy Strength of an ionic bond; the energy required for the separation of the ions in 1 mole of a crystal to an infinite distance from each other. Alternative name: lattice enthalpy.

launch window Period of time during which a rocket may be launched on a particular **trajectory**. The term was previously applied only to spacecraft but is now used by the military to describe opportunities for much smaller projectiles such as missiles.

law In science, simple statement or mathematical expression for the generalization of results relating to a particular phenomenon or known facts. There are articles on many scientific laws listed under their individual names in this dictionary (*e.g.*, **conservation of mass, law of**).

LDR Abbreviation of **light-dependent resistor**.

lead-acid accumulator Rechargable **electrolytic cell** (battery) that has positive electrodes of lead (IV) oxide (PbO_2), negative electrodes of lead, and a solution of sulphuric acid as the electrolyte.

lead equivalent Factor that compares any form of shielding against radioactivity to the thickness of lead that would provide the same measure of protection.

Le Chatelier's principle If a change occurs in one of the factors (such as temperature or pressure) under which a system is in equilibrium, the system will tend to adjust itself so as to counteract the effect of that change. It was named after French physicist Henri le Chatelier (1850–1936). Alternative name: Le Chatelier-Braun principle.

Leclanché cell Primary cell that has a zinc cathode and carbon anode dipping into an electrolyte of ammonium chloride solution. A porous pot of crushed carbon and manganese (IV) oxide (managanese dioxide) surrounds the anode to prevent **polarization**. It is the basis of the **dry cell** used in most batteries. It was named after the French chemist Georges Leclanché (1839–1882).

LED Abbreviation of **light-emitting diode**.

LEED Abbreviation of **low-energy electron diffraction**.

left-hand rule Rule that relates the directions of current, magnetic field and movement in an electric motor. If the left hand is held with the thumb, first and second fingers at right angles, the thumb indicates the direction of movement, the first finger the direction of the magnetic field and the second finger the direction of current flow. Alternative name: Fleming left-hand rule, after the British physicist Ambrose Fleming (1849–1945).

lens Any device for focusing or modifying the direction of a beam of rays (usually light) passing through it. By analogy also a current-carrying coil that focuses a beam of electrons (as in an **electron microscope**).

Lenz's law When a wire moves in a **magnetic field,** the electric current induced in the wire generates a magnetic field that tends to oppose the motion. It was named after the Russian physicist Heinrich Lenz (1804–1865).

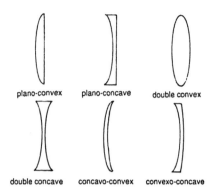

Various types of lenses

lepton Subatomic particle that does not interact strongly with other particles, *e.g.*, an electron. *See also* **hadron**.

lever Rigid bar supported or pivoted at some point (called the fulcrum) along its length. An effort applied at one point on the bar can move a load at another point; a lever is thus a simple machine. Every lever belongs to one of three classes or orders, depending on whether the fulcrum is between the load and effort (class 1), or the load and effort are on the same side of the fulcrum, with the load nearer the fulcrum (class 2) or the effort nearer the fulcrum (class 3).

levorotatory Describing a compound with **optical activity** that causes the plane of polarized light to rotate in a counterclockwise direction. Indicated by the prefix (-)- or *l*-.

Leyden jar Original and obsolete form of **capacitor**, named after the Dutch town (now Leiden).

light Visible part of the **electromagnetic spectrum**, of wavelengths between about 400 and 760 nanometers.

light, speed of *See* **speed of light**.

light-dependent resistor

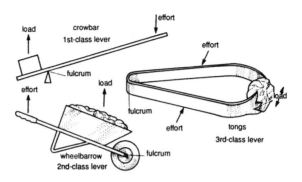

The three classes of levers

light-dependent resistor (LDR) Resistor made from a **semiconductor** (*e.g.*, cadmium sulphide, selenium) whose resistance decreases when light falls on it.

light-emitting diode (LED) Semiconducting **diode** that gives off light, used for displaying numerals and letters in calculators, watches and other equipment.

lightning Gigantic electric spark within a cloud, between clouds or between a cloud and the earth. The spark occurs when clouds become highly electrically charged, different areas of one cloud often having an opposite charge.

lightning conductor Metal rod with its upper end projecting to attract lighting and its lower end buried in the ground. It is used to protect buildings against lightning strikes.

light pen Computer **input device**, used in association with special software, that enables an operator to write or draw on a VDU screen more or less as if using an ordinary pen.

light-year Unit of distance in astronomy, the distance light travels in one year (about 9.4650×10^{12} km, or 5.88×10^{12} miles). The nearest star to the sun, Proxima Centauri, is approximately 4 light-years away.

limiting friction Maximum value of a frictional force.

linear absorption coefficient Measure of a medium's ability to absorb a beam of radiation passing through it, but not to scatter or diffuse it.

linear accelerator Apparatus for accelerating charged particles.

linear attenuation coefficient Measure of a medium's ability to diffuse and absorb a beam of radiation passing through it.

linear energy transfer (LET) Linear rate of energy dispersion of separate particles of radiation when they penetrate an absorbing medium.

linear momentum Product of the mass (m) of a moving object and its velocity (v); mv.

linear motor Type of **induction motor** in which the "rotor" travels along a rail that acts as the stator.

line printer Comparatively fast computer **output device** that prints out **data** one whole line at a time.

line spectrum Spectrum that consists of separate lines of definite wavelengths. The spectral lines are produced by the excited electrons of atoms falling back to lower **energy levels** with the emission of photons.

liquefaction of gases All gases can be liquefied by a combination of cooling and compression. The greater the pressure, the less the gas needs to be cooled, but there is for each gas a certain **critical temperature** below which it must be cooled before it can be liquefied.

liquid Fluid that, without changing its volume, takes the shape of all or the lower part of its container. According to the **kinetic theory**, the molecules in a liquid are not bound together as rigidly as those in a solid but neither are they as free to move as those of a gas.

liquid crystal Compound that is liquid at room temperature and atmospheric pressure but shows characteristics normally expected only from solid crystalline substances. Large groups of its molecules maintain their mobility but nevertheless also retain a form of structural relationship. Some liquid crystals change color according to the temperature.

liquid-crystal display (LCD) **Digital display** based on liquid crystal cells used in calculators, watches and other equipment.

Lissajous' figure Plane curve formed by the combination of two or more simple periodic motions. It was named after the French physicist Jules Lissajous (1822–1880). Alternative name: Lissajous' circle.

liter (1) Unit of volume in the metric system, defined as 1 dm^3, *i.e.*, 1,000 cm^3 (formerly defined as the volume of 1 kg of water at 4°C). 1 liter = 1.7598 pints.

Lloyd's mirror Device for producing interference bands of contrasting brightness or darkness. A plane glass plate (acting as a mirror) is illuminated by monochromatic light from a slit parallel to the plate. Interference occurs between direct light from the slit and that reflected from the plate. It was named after the British physicist Humphrey Lloyd (1800–1881).

local oscillator Oscillator that supplies the **radio frequency** oscillation with which the received wave is combined in a **superheterodyne** radio receiver.

lodestone Naturally occurring magnetic oxide of iron, a piece of which was reputedly used (by being suspended on a thread) as a primitive compass. Alternative names: loadstone, magnetite.

logarithmic scale Nonlinear scale of measurement. For common logarithms (to the base 10), an increase of one unit represents a tenfold increase in the quantity measured.

logic In electronic data-processing systems, the principles that define the interactions of data in the form of physical entities.

logic gate Electronic switching circuit that gives an output only when specified input conditions are met. It is part of a **computer**

that performs a particular logical operation (*e.g.*, "AND," "OR," "NOT," etc.). Alternative names: logic circuit, logic element.

longitude Imaginary line that passes around Earth through both poles. The angular distance around the globe is 360°, which is measured as 180° east of Greenwich (designated 0°) and 180° west of Greenwich. Using longitude in combination with **latitude**, any position on Earth's surface can be denoted. Alternative name: meridian.

longitudinal wave Elastic wave in which the particles of a medium vibrate in the direction of propagation.

Lorentz-Fitzgerald contraction Contraction in the length of a moving object in its direction of motion at near the velocity of light and relative to the frame of reference from which measurements are made, proposed independently by the Dutch physicist Hendrik Lorentz (1853–1928) and the Irish physicist George Fitzgerald (1851–1901). Alternative names: Lorentz contraction; Fitzgerald-Lorentz contraction.

Lorentz relation Alternative name for **Widemann-Franz law**.

Lorentz transformation Set of equations for correlating space and time coordinates in two frames of reference.

loudness Property of sound determined by the **amplitude** of the sound waves, usually expressed in **decibels**.

loudspeaker Device for converting electrical impulses into audible sound, usually by making a **solenoid** vibrate a conical diaphragm.

low-energy electron diffraction Electron diffraction that uses low-energy electrons, which are strongly diffracted by surface layers of atoms.

low frequency (LF) Radio frequency of between 30 and 300 kHz.

lubricant Any substance used to reduce friction between surfaces in contact; *e.g.*, oil, graphite, molybdenum disulphide, silicone grease.

lumen SI unit of luminous flux, equal to the amount of light emitted by source of 1 candela through unit solid angle.

luminance Measure of surface brightness expressed as the luminous flux per unit solid angle per unit projected area.

luminescence Emission of light by a substance without any appreciable rise in temperature. *See* **fluorescence; incandescence; phosphorescence.**

luminosity Brightness, *e.g.*, of an image or a star.

luminous intensity Amount of light emitted in a given direction per second in unit solid angle by a point source.

lux SI unit of illumination, equal to one lumen per square meter. Alternative name: meter-candle.

Lyman series Series of lines in the ultraviolet **spectrum** of hydrogen. It was named after the American physicist Theodore Lyman (1874–1954).

lyophilic Possessing an affinity for liquids.

lyophobic Liquid-repellent, having no attraction for liquids.

M

machine Device for doing **work** in which a small **force** (the effort) overcomes a larger force (the load); *e.g.,* in the simplest case, levers and pulleys, the inclined plane and the wheel-and-axle. This mechanical definition can be extended to also include electrical devices, such as a transformer. *See also* **efficiency; mechanical advantage; velocity ratio**.

machine code Code in which instructions are given to a **computer**. Many computer languages (used for **programs**) have to be translated into machine code before they can be "understood" by a computer.

Mach number Indication of the speed of an object in relation to the speed of sound in a particular medium (1,229 km/h in air at sea level), which is given the value Mach 1. An aircraft traveling at Mach 2 is flying at twice the speed of sound.

macro- Prefix meaning large or long in size or duration.

magnet Object possessing the property of **magnetism**, either permanently (a permanent magnet, made of a ferromagnetic material) or temporarily under the influence of another magnet or the magnetic field associated with an electric current (an **electromagnet**). *See also* **paramagnetism**.

magnetic amplifier Transducer so arranged that a small controlling direct current input can produce large changes in coupled alternating current circuits.

magnetic circuit Completely closed path described by a given set of lines of **magnetic flux**.

magnetic core Computer storage device consisting of a ferromagnetic ring wound with wires; a current flowing in the wires polarizes the core, which can therefore adopt one of two states (making it a bistable device).

magnetic declination Angle by which north as shown by a magnetic compass (magnetic north) deviates from **true north**. The position of magnetic north is subject to significant variation with time, and for this reason magnetic declination is not a constant factor.

magnetic dip *See* **dip**.

magnetic disk Device for direct-access storage and retrieval of data, used in computers and similar systems. It consists of a rotatable flexible or rigid plastic disk (*i.e.*, a floppy or hard disk) coated on one or both surfaces with magnetic material, such as iron oxide. Data is stored or retrieved through one or more **read-write heads**. Alternative name: magnetic disc.

magnetic domain Group of atoms with aligned magnetic moments that occur in a **ferromagnetic** material. There are many randomly oriented domains in a permanent **magnet**.

magnetic drum Computer storage device consisting of a rotatable drum coated with magnetic material, such as iron oxide. Data is stored or retrieved through one or more **read-write heads**.

magnetic element *See* **geomagnetism**.

magnetic field Field of force in the space around the magnetic poles of a **magnet**.

magnetic field strength Alternative name for **magnetic intensity**.

magnetic flux Measure of the total size of a **magnetic field**, defined as the scalar product of the flux density and the area. Its SI unit is the weber.

magnetic flux density Product of **magnetic intensity** and **permeability**. Its SI unit is the tesla (formerly weber m^{-2}).

magnetic induction In a magnetic material, magnetization induced in it, *e.g.*, by placing it in the electromagnetic field of a current-carrying coil or by stroking it with a permanent **magnet**.

magnetic intensity Magnitude of a magnetic field. Its SI unit is the ampere m^{-2}. Alternative names: magnetic field strength, magnetizing force.

magnetic lens Arrangement of electromagnets used to focus a beam of charged particles (*e.g.*, electrons in an **electron microscope**).

magnetic mirror Region of high magnetic field strength that reflects particles from a **plasma** back into a magnetic bottle. *See also* **fusion reactor**.

magnetic moment Property possessed by an individual atom or molecule, a moving charge, a permanent magnet, or a current-carrying coil, used as a measure of its magnetic strength. Multiplied by the magnetic induction it equals the torque (turning force) on the magnet.

magnetic monopole Theoretically possible, but so far unobserved, single **magnetic pole**.

magnetic north Point on Earth's surface toward which a magnetic compass points. The exact location of magnetic north varies seasonally, and from year to year. *See also* **magnetic declination; true north**.

magnetic pole 1. One of the two points, called north and south, to and from which a **magnetic field** appears to radiate. Unless deliberately made otherwise, *e.g.*, in a horseshoe magnet, the magnet poles tend to occur at opposite sides of any object exhibiting magnetism. 2. Position on Earth to or from which a magnetized needle (a compass) points. The positions of the magnetic poles vary over a period of time and do not coincide with the geographic poles. The angular difference between the directions of magnetic north and true north is the **magnetic declination**. *See also* **dip**.

magnetic storm Local disturbances in Earth's magnetic field that can disrupt **telecommunications** and that are probably caused by gusts of charged particles emanating from the sun.

magnetic susceptibility Difference between **relative permeability** and unity; equal to the intensity of magnetization divided by the applied field.

magnetic tape Medium for the storage of electronic signals by magnetizing particles (of *e.g.*, iron oxide) in a coating on plastic tape. It is used in (audio) tape recorders, video recorders and computers.

magnetism Presence of magnetic properties in materials. **Diamagnetism** is a weak effect common to all substances and results from the orbital motion of electrons. In certain substances this is masked by a stronger effect, **paramagnetism**, due to electron spin. Some paramagnetic materials such as iron also display **ferromagnetism** and are permanently magnetic.

magnetization Difference between the ratio of the **magnetic induction** to the **permeability** and the **magnetic intensity**; its SI unit is the ampere m^{-1}. It represents departure from randomness of **magnetic domains**.

magnetohydrodynamics Branch of physics that deals with the behavior of a conducting fluid under the influence of a **magnetic flux**.

magneton Unit for the **magnetic moment** of an electron. Alternative name: Bohr-magneton.

magnetron Electronic valve that is used to provide pulsed emissions in **microwave** telecommunications, **radar** transmitters, and microwave cookers.

magnification In optics, the ratio y'/y, where y is the height of an object perpendicular to the optical axis and y' is the corresponding height of its magnified image. For a single lens this is equivalent to the ratio of the image distance to the object distance.

Mallory cell Alternative name for **mercury cell**.

manganin Alloy of copper with manganese and nickel that exhibits high electrical **resistance** and is used in resistors.

manometer Device for measuring fluid pressure.

mascon Short form of mass concentration, one of many unexplained areas of high gravity that have been detected on the moon's surface.

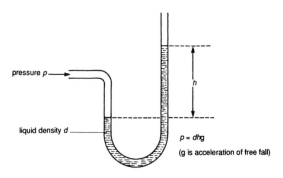

$$p = dhg$$
(g is acceleration of free fall)

Simple liquid manometer measures gas pressure

maser Device that produces narrow **microwave** beams, and which operates on the same principle as a **laser**. The name is an acronym for "microwave amplification by stimulated emission of radiation."

mass Quantity of matter in an object. The SI unit of mass is the **kilogram**. *See also* **weight**.

mass decrement *See* **mass defect**.

mass defect 1. Difference between the mass of an atomic **nucleus** and the masses of the particles that make it up, equivalent to the **binding energy** of the nucleus (expressed in mass units). 2. Mass of an **isotope** minus its mass number. Alternative names: mass decrement, mass excess.

mass-energy equation Deduction from Einstein's special theory of relativity that all energy has mass; $E = mc^2$, where E is the energy, m is the amount of mass, and c the speed of light.

mass number (A) Total number of **protons** and **neutrons** in an atomic **nucleus**. Alternative name: nucleon number. *See also* **isotope**.

mass spectrograph Vacuum system in which positive rays of charged atoms (**ions**) are passed through electric and magnetic fields so as to separate them in order of their charge-to-mass ratios on a photographic plate. It measures **relative atomic masses** of **isotopes** with precision.

mass spectrometer **Mass spectrograph** that uses electrical methods rather than photographic ones to detect charged particles.

mass spectrum Indication of the distribution in mass, or in mass-to-charge ratio, of ionized atoms or molecules produced by a **mass spectrograph**.

matter Substance that occupies space and has the property of **inertia**. These two characteristics distinguish matter from energy, the various forms of which make up the rest of the material universe.

maximum and minimum thermometer *See* **thermometer, maximum and minimum**.

maxwell CGS unit of magnetic flux, the SI unit being the weber. 1 maxwell = 10^{-8} weber. It was named after the British physicist James Clerk Maxwell (1831–1879).

Maxwell-Boltzmann distribution Law that describes the distribution of energy among molecules of a gas in thermal equilibrium.

mean free path Average distance that a gas molecule moves between two successive collisions with other molecules.

mean free time Average time between collisions of 1. gas molecules; 2. electrons and impurity atoms in a **semiconductor**.

mean life 1. Average time for which the unstable **nucleus** of a radioisotope exists before decaying. 2. Average time of survival of an elementary particle, ion, etc., in a given medium or of a charge carrier in a **semiconductor**.

mean solar day Average value over a year of the solar day, the constant time between two transits of the sun across the meridian. It equals 24 hours.

mechanical advantage (MA) For a simple machine, the ratio of the load L (output force) to the effort E (input force); *i.e.*, $MA = L/E$. Alternative name: force ratio.

mechanics Study of the interaction between matter and the forces acting on it. Its three divisions are **kinematics** (concerned with acceleration, velocity, etc.), **dynamics** (concerned with forces acting on objects in motion) and **statics** (concerned with forces that do not produce motion).

mega- Metric prefix meaning million times; x 10^6 (*e.g.*, megahertz).

megahertz (MHz) Unit of frequency of one million **hertz**.

megaton Measure of the explosive power of a nuclear explosion or warhead, equivalent to a million tons of TNT.

melting point Temperature at which a solid begins to liquefy, a fixed (and therefore characteristic) temperature for a pure substance.

memory Part of a computer that stores data and instructions (programs), usually referring to the immediate access store. *See also* **random access memory** (RAM); **read-only memory** (ROM).

meniscus Curved surface of a liquid where it is in contact with a solid. The effect is due to **surface tension**.

mensuration Science of a measurement.

mercury arc

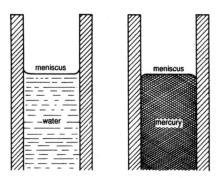

Shape of a meniscus depends on the liquid

mercury arc Bright blue-green light obtained from an electric discharge through mercury vapor.

mercury cell 1. **Electrolytic cell** that has a **cathode** made of mercury. 2. Dry cell that has a mercury electrode. Alternative name: Mallory cell.

mercury-vapor lamp Lamp that uses a **mercury arc** in a quartz tube; it produces **ultraviolet radiation.**

meridian Line of **longitude,** a great circle that passes through the poles.

meson Member of a group of unstable **elementary particles** with masses intermediate between those of **electrons** and **nucleons,** and with positive, negative or zero charge. Mesons are emitted by **nuclei** that have been bombarded by high-energy electrons.

meta- Prefix that generally indicates the concept of change, and which may mean after or beyond; *e.g.,* metastable.

metal Any of a group of **elements** and their alloys with general properties of strength, hardness and the ability to conduct heat and electricity (because of the presence of free electrons). Most have high melting points and can be polished to a shiny finish.

Metallic elements (about 80 percent of the total) tend to form **cations**. *See also* **metalloid**.

metal fatigue Weakness in a metal caused by a long period of stress, which can cause cracks and disintegration, *e.g.*, in the structure of aircraft.

metalloid Element with physical properties resembling those of metals and chemical properties typical of nonmetals (*e.g.*, arsenic, germanium, selenium). Many metalloids are used in **semiconductors**.

metastatic Describing **electrons** that leave an orbital shell, either entering another shell or being absorbed into the nucleus.

meter (m) SI unit of length 1 m = 39.37 inches.

meter-candle Alternative name for **lux**.

metric prefix Any of various numerical prefixes used in the **metric system**. *See* **units**.

metric system Decimal-based system of units. *See* **SI units**.

metric ton Alternative name for **tonne**.

MHD Abbreviation of **magnetohydrodynamics**.

micro- 1. Metric prefix meaning a millionth; x 10^{-6} (*e.g.*, microfarad). It is sometimes represented by the Greek letter μ (*e.g.*, μF). 2. General prefix meaning small (*e.g.*, next three entries).

microbalance Balance capable of weighing very small masses (*e.g.*, down to 10^{-5} mg).

microcomputer Small computer. Alternative name: personal computer (PC).

microelectronics Branch of electronics that is concerned with the design, production and application of electronic components, circuits and devices of extremely small dimensions.

micron

micron (μ) Former name for the micrometer; 10^{-6} m.

microphone Device for converting sound energy into electrical energy. There are various types. In a moving-coil microphone, a coil connected to a diaphragm (vibrated by sound waves) moves in a magnetic field, generating a current in the coil by **electromagnetic induction**. In a moving-iron microphone, a small piece of iron is vibrated by a diaphragm in a magnetic field, varying the field and inducing a current in a surrounding coil. In a carbon microphone, a vibrating metallic diaphragm compresses carbon granules, thereby altering their resistance. In a crystal microphone, vibrations are transmitted to a piezoelectric crystal that generates a varying electric field.

microprocessor *See* **computer**.

microscope Instrument that produces magnified images of structures invisible to the naked eye. There are two major optical types: the simple microscope, consisting of one short focal-length convex lens giving a virtual image, and the compound microscope, consisting of two short focal-length convex lenses that combine to give high magnification. Highest magnifications are produced by an **electron microscope**.

microwave Electromagnetic radiation with a wavelength in the approximate range 1 mm to 0.3 m, *i.e.*, between **infrared radiation** and **radio waves**.

microwave spectroscopy Study of atomic and/or molecular resonances in the **microwave** region.

mil 1. A milliliter. 2. One-thousandth of an inch, equivalent to 0.0254 mm.

mile Unit of length equal to 1,760 yards or 5,280 feet. 1 mile = 1.60934 kilometers. A nautical mile is 6,080 feet (= 1.85318 km).

milli- Metric prefix meaning a thousandth; x 10^{-3} (*e.g.*, milligram).

millibar (mbar) Thousandth of a **bar**, a common unit of atmospheric pressure in meteorology.

milligram (mg) Thousandth of a gram.

milliliter (ml) Thousandth of a liter, equivalent to a cubic centimeter (cc or cm^3).

millimeter (mm) Thousandth of a meter, equal to a tenth of a centimeter. 1 mm = 0.03937 inches.

millimeter of mercury (mmHg) Unit of pressure, equal to 1/760 atmospheres.

minute 1. Unit of time equal to 1/60 of an hour. 2. Unit of angular measure equal to 1/60 of a degree. Both types of minutes are made up of 60 seconds.

mirage False image sometimes observed in deserts and polar regions. It is caused by light reflecting off the upper surface of a layer of very hot (or very cold) air near the ground.

mirror Optical device that produces reflection, generally having surfaces that are plane, spherical, paraboloidal, ellipsoidal or aspheric. Concave mirrors are hollow, convex mirrors are domed outward.

mobility In electronics: 1. Freedom of particles to move, either randomly, in a field or under the influence of forces. 2. Average drift velocity of charge carriers (per unit electric field) in a **semiconductor.**

modem Acronym of modulator/demodulator, a device for transmitting computer **data** over long distances (*e.g.*, by telephone line).

moderator Material used to slow down **neutrons** in a nuclear reactor (so that they can be captured and initiate **nuclear fission**); *e.g.*, water, heavy water or graphite.

modulation In radio transmission, change of amplitude or frequency of a carrier wave by the signal being transmitted. *See* **amplitude modulation; frequency modulation.**

modulus of elasticity *See* **elastic modulus**.

moiré pattern Interference fringes formed when light passes through two or more fine gratings. A similar effect is created by the tiny dots in a printed (colored) half-tone photograph when the screen angles are too close.

molar conductivity Electrical conductivity of an electrolyte with a

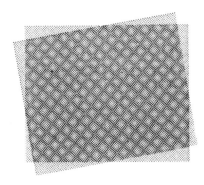

Moiré pattern formed from two sets of regular dots

concentration of 1 mole of solute per liter of solution. Expressed in siemens cm^2 $mole^{-1}$.

molar heat capacity Heat required to increase the temperature of 1 mole of a substance by 1 kelvin. Expressed in joules K^{-1} mol^{-1}.

molar volume Volume occupied by 1 mole of a substance under specified conditions.

mole (mol) SI unit of amount of substance. In chemistry, it is the amount of a substance in grams that corresponds to its molecular weight, or the amount that contains particles equal in number to the **Avogadro constant**. Alternative name: gram-molecule.

molecular distillation Distillation at extremely low pressures. Alternative name: high-vacuum distillation.

molecular orbital Region in space occupied by a pair of **electrons** that form a covalent bond in a **molecule**, formed by the overlap of two **atomic orbitals**.

molecular sieve Method of separating substances by trapping (absorbing) the molecules of one within cavities of another, usually a natural or synthetic zeolite. Molecular sieves are used in ion exchange, desalination and as supports for catalysts.

molecular spectrum *See* **spectrum**.

molecule Group of atoms held together in fixed proportions by chemical bonds; the fundamental unit of a chemical compound. The simplest molecules are diatomic molecules, consisting of two atoms (*e.g.*, O_2, HCl); the most complex are biochemicals and macromolecules (such as cellulose, rubber, starch and synthetic plastics).

moment of force About an axis, the product of the perpendicular distance of the axis from the line of action of the force and the component of the force in the plane perpendicular to the axis. It has a turning effect (torque). *See also* **couple**.

moment of inertia (I) Sum of the products of the mass of each particle of a body about an axis and the square of its perpendicular distance from the axis (its radius of gyration).

momentum (*p*) Product of the mass *m* and velocity *v* of a moving object; *i.e.*, $p = mv$. It is a vector quantity directed through the center of mass of the object in the direction of motion. When objects collide, the total momentum before impact is the same as total momentum after impact.

mono- Prefix meaning one (*e.g.*, monoclinic).

monochromatic light Light of a single **wavelength**.

monochromator *See* **spectrometer**.

monoclinic Crystal form in which all three axes are unequal, with one of them perpendicular to the other two, which intersect at an angle inclined at other than a right angle.

Moseley's law The X-ray spectrum of an element can be divided into several distinct line series: K, L, M and N. The law states that for certain elements the square root of the frequency f of the characteristic X-rays of one of these series is directly proportional to the element's **atomic number** Z. It was named after the British physicist Henry Moseley (1887–1915).

Mössbauer effect Absorption of momentum of an atom by the whole crystal lattice because it is so firmly bound that it cannot recoil after its **nucleus** has emitted a gamma ray **photon**. It was named after the German physicist Rudolf Mössbauer (1929–).

motor, electric *See* **electric motor.**

motor effect A conductor carrying a direct current (d.c.) in a magnetic field tends to move, which is the principle by which an **electric motor** works. *See* **left-hand rule.**

motor generator Motor supplied at one voltage frequency-coupled to a generator that provides a different voltage/frequency.

moving-coil microphone *See* **microphone.**

moving-iron microphone *See* **microphone.**

multimeter Instrument that can be used as a galvanometer, ammeter and voltmeter.

multiplication constant In a nuclear reactor, the ratio of the total number of **neutrons** produced by fission in a given time to the number absorbed or escaping in the same period. Alternative name: multiplication factor.

multiplier One of a set of resistors that can be used in series with a **voltmeter** to vary its range.

muon Subatomic particle, a type of **lepton**, that participates in weak interactions.

mutarotation Change in the **optical activity** of a solution containing photo-active substances, such as sugars.

myopia Alternative name for **nearsightedness**.

N

nano- Prefix meaning a thousand-millionth; x 10^{-9}. *E.g.,* 1 nanosecond is 10^{-9} s.

nanometer Thousand-millionth of a meter; 10^{-9} m. It is the usual unit for wavelengths of light and interatomic bond lengths in chemistry.

natural abundance Relative proportion of the various **isotopes** in a naturally occurring sample of an element.

natural frequency When a vibrating system is displaced from its neutral position it oscillates about that position with a natural frequency characteristic of the system. *See also* **resonance.**

nautical mile Distance used at sea. In Britain 1 nautical mile = 6,080 feet; the international definition is 1,852 meters.

near infrared or **ultraviolet** Parts of the infrared or ultraviolet regions of the **electromagnetic spectrum** that are close to the visible region.

nearsightedness Visual defect in which the eyeball is too long (front to back) so that rays of light entering the **eye** from distant objects are brought to a focus in front of the retina. It can be corrected with spectacles or contact lenses with diverging (concave) lenses. Alternative name: myopia.

negative feedback *See* **feedback.**

neon tube Gas-discharge tube that contains neon at low pressure, the color of the glow being red.

Nernst effect When heat flows through a strip of metal in a magnetic field, the direction of heat flow being across the lines of force, an e.m.f. is developed perpendicular to both the flow and the lines. It was named after the German physical chemist Walther Nernst (1864–1941).

Nernst heat theorem If a chemical change occurs between pure crystalline solids at a temperature of absolute zero, the entropy of the final substance equals that of the initial substances.

network System of interconnected points and their connections; *e.g.,* a grid of electricity supply lines or a set of interconnected terminals online to one or more computers.

neutral Having neither positive nor negative electrical charge; *e.g.,* a **neutron** is a neutral subatomic particle.

neutrino Uncharged subatomic particle with zero rest mass, a type of **lepton**, that interacts very weakly with other particles.

neutron Uncharged particle that is a constituent of the atomic **nucleus,** having a rest mass of 1.67492×10^{-27} kg (similar to that of a **proton**). Free neutrons are unstable and disintegrate by **beta decay** to a proton and an **electron**; outside the nucleus they have a mean life of about 12 minutes.

neutron diffraction Technique for determining the crystal structure of solids by diffraction of a beam of **neutrons.** Similar in principle to electron diffraction, it can be used as a substitute for **X-ray crystallography**.

neutron excess Alternative name for **isotopic number.**

neutron flux Product of the number of free neutrons per unit volume and their mean speed. Alternative name: neutron flux density.

neutron number Number of neutrons in an atomic nucleus, the difference between the **nucleon number** of an element and its **atomic number**.

newton (N) SI unit of **force**, defined as the force that provides a
mass of 1 kg with an **acceleration** of 1 ms^{-2}. It was named
after the British mathematician and physicist Isaac Newton
(1642–1727).

Newtonian fluid Fluid in which the amount of strain is
proportional both to the stress and to the time. The constant of
proportionality is known as the coefficient of viscosity.

Newtonian mechanics System of mechanics that relies on
Newton's laws of motion and is applicable to objects moving
at speeds relative to the observer that are small compared to the
speed of light. Objects moving near to the speed of light require
an approach based on relativistic mechanics (*see* **relativity**), in
which the mass of the object changes with its speed.

newton meter Instrument for measuring a **force** in newtons
(*e.g.*, spring balance).

Newton's formula For a lens, the distances p and q between two
conjugate points and their respective foci (f) are related by
$pq = f^2$.

Newton's law of cooling Rate of loss of heat from an object is
proportional to the excess temperature of the object over the
temperature of its surroundings.

Newton's law of gravitation Force F of attraction between two
objects of masses m_1, m_2 separated by a distance x is given by
$F = Gm_1m_2 /x^2$; G is the gravitational constant and has a value
of 6.6732 x 10^{-11} Nm^2 kg^{-2}. Alternative name: law of universal
gravitation.

Newton's laws of motion Three laws of motion on which
Newtonian mechanics is based. 1. An object continues in a
state of rest or uniform motion in a straight line unless it is
acted upon by external forces. 2. Rate of change of momentum
of a moving object is proportional to and in the same direction
as the force acting on it. 3. If one object exerts a force on
another, there is an equal and opposite force, called a reaction,

114

exerted on the first object by the second. Alternative name: Newton's law of force.

Newton's rings Circular **interference** fringes formed in a thin gap between two reflective media, *e.g.*, between a lens and a glass plate with which the lens is in contact. There is a central dark spot around which there are concentric dark rings.

nickel-iron accumulator Rechargeable **electrolytic cell** (battery) with a positive electrode of nickel oxide and a negative electrode of iron, in a potassium hydroxide electrolyte. Alternative name: Edison accumulator, NiFe cell.

NiFe cell Alternative name for **nickel-iron accumulator.**

NMR Abbreviation of nuclear magnetic resonance, an effect observed when radio-frequency radiation is absorbed by matter. NMR spectroscopy is used in chemistry for the study of molecular structure. It has also been introduced as a technique of diagnostic medicine.

node Stationary point (*i.e.*, point with zero amplitude) on a **standing wave.**

noise Sound (or other radiation) consisting of a mixture of random and unrelated frequencies. If all the frequencies in a range are represented, it is called white noise.

nonmetal Substance that does not have the properties of a **metal.** Nonmetallic **elements** are usually gases (*e.g.*, nitrogen, halogen, noble gases) or low-melting point solids (*e.g.*, phosphorus, sulfur, iodine). They have poor electrical and thermal **conductivity**.

non-Newtonian fluid Fluid that consists of two or more phases at the same time. The coefficient of viscosity is not a constant but is a function of the rate at which the fluid is sheared as well as of the relative concentration of the phases.

normal Line at right angles to a surface (*e.g.*, a mirror or block of glass), from which angles of incidence, reflection and refraction are measured.

NTP

NTP Abbreviation of normal temperature and pressure. *See also* **standard temperature and pressure** (STP).

n-type conductivity Electrical conductivity caused by the flow of **electrons** in a **semiconductor**.

nuclear barrier Region of high potential energy that a charged particle must pass through in order to enter or leave an atomic nucleus.

nuclear energy Energy released during a **nuclear fission** or **fusion** process.

nuclear fission Splitting of an atomic nucleus into two or more fragments of comparable size, usually as the result of the capture of a slow, or thermal, **neutron** by the nucleus. It is normally accompanied by the emission of further neutrons or **gamma rays**, and large amounts of energy. The neutrons can continue the process as a **chain reaction,** so that it becomes the source of energy in a nuclear reactor or an atomic bomb. It may also be the "trigger" for **nuclear fusion** in a hydrogen bomb.

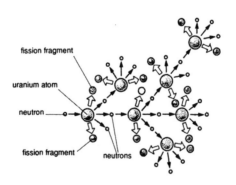

Nuclear fission splits heavy atoms

nuclear force Strong force that operates during interactions between certain subatomic particles. It holds together the **protons** and **neutrons** in an atomic **nucleus.**

nuclear fusion Reaction between light atomic nuclei in which a heavier nucleus is formed with the release of large amounts of energy. This process is the basis of the production of energy in stars and in the hydrogen bomb, which makes use of the fusion of **isotopes** of hydrogen to form helium.

nuclear isomerism Property exhibited by nuclei with the same **mass number** and **atomic number** but different radioactive properties.

nuclear magnetic resonance (NMR) *See* **NMR**.

nuclear power Power obtained by the conversion of heat from a **nuclear reactor**, usually into electrical energy.

nuclear reaction Reaction that occurs between an atomic **nucleus** and a bombarding particle or photon, leading to the formation of a new nucleus and the possible ejection of one or more particles with the release of energy.

nuclear reactor Assembly in which controlled **nuclear fission** takes place (as a **chain reaction**) with the release of heat energy. There are various types, including a **breeder reactor**, **gas-cooled reactor** and **pressurized water reactor**.

nuclear transmutation Conversion of an element into another by **nuclear reaction**.

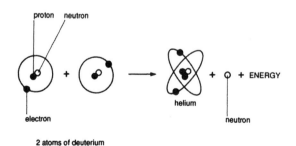

Nuclear fusion combines light atoms

nuclear waste Radioactive by-products of a **nuclear reactor** or from the mining and extraction of nuclear fuels.

nuclear weapon Weapon whose destructive power comes from the release of energy accompanying **nuclear fission** or **fusion;** *e.g.,* an atomic bomb or hydrogen bomb.

nucleon Comparatively massive particle in an atomic **nucleus;** a **proton** or **neutron.**

nucleonics Practical applications of nuclear science and the techniques associated with these applications.

nucleon number Total number of **neutrons** and **protons** in an atomic nucleus. *See* **mass number.**

nucleus The most massive, central part of the atom of an element, having a positive charge given by Ze, where Z is the **atomic number** of the element and e the charge on an **electron**. It is composed of chiefly **protons** and (except for hydrogen) **neutrons,** and is surrounded by orbiting **electrons**. *See also* **isotope.**

nuclide Atomic nucleus, defined by its **atomic number** and **neutron number.**

null method Any measuring system that establishes an unknown value from other known values when a particular instrument registers zero, *e.g.,* a **potentiometer**. Alternative name: zero method.

nutation Periodic variation in the axis of a spinning object, *e.g.,* a **gyroscope**.

O

object With a mirror, lens or optical instrument, the source of light rays that form an **image**.

objective Lens of an optical system (*e.g.*, microscope, telescope) that is nearest the object.

OCR Abbreviation of **optical character reader.**

octa-/octo- Prefix meaning eight.

octet Stable group of eight **electrons**; the outer electron configuration of most rare gases, and the arrangement achieved by the atoms of other elements as a result of most cases of chemical combination between them. Alternative name: electron octet.

odd-even nucleus Atomic **nucleus** with an odd number of **protons** and an even number of **neutrons**.

odd-odd nucleus Atomic **nucleus** with an odd number of both **protons** and **neutrons**.

oersted C.g.s. unit of electromagnetic field strength, replaced in the SI system by the ampere per meter. It was named after the Danish physicist Hans Oersted (1777–1851).

ohm ω Practical unit of electrical resistance. It is the resistance of a conductor in which the current is 1 ampere when a potential difference of 1 volt is applied across it. It was named after the German physicist Georg Ohm (1787–1854).

Ohm's law Relationship stating that the **voltage** across a conductor is equal to the product of the **current** flowing through it and its **resistance**. It is written $V = IR$, where V is voltage, I current and R resistance.

oligo- Prefix that denotes small or few in number.

omega-minus Negatively charged **elementary particle**, the heaviest **hyperon**.

online Describing part of a **computer** (*e.g.*, an **input device**) that is linked directly to and under the control of the **central processor**.

opaque Not allowing a wave motion (*e.g.*, light, sound, X-rays) to pass; not transmitting light, not transparent.

optic Concerning the **eye** and vision.

optical activity Phenomenon exhibited by some chemical compounds that, when placed in the path of a beam of plane-polarized light, are capable of rotating the plane of polarization to the left (**levorotatory**) or right (**dextrorotatory**). Alternative name: optical rotation.

optical axis Line that passes through the **optical center** and the **center of curvature** of a spherical **lens** or **mirror**. Alternative name: principal axis.

optical center Point at the center of a **lens** through which a ray continues straight on and undeviated.

optical character reader (OCR) Computer **input device** that "reads" printer or written **alphanumeric** characters and feeds the information into a computer system.

optical glass Very pure glass free from streaks and bubbles, used for lenses, etc.

optical rotation Alternative name for **optical activity**.

optical telescope Instrument used to observe heavenly bodies by the light that they emit. It consists of lenses or mirrors, or both, that make distant objects appear nearer and larger.

optics Branch of physics concerned with the study of light.

orbit 1. In astronomy and space science, the path of one heavenly body moving around another (*e.g.*, Earth around the sun, or the moon around Earth), or the path of an artificial satellite around a heavenly body. 2. In atomic physics, the path of motion of an **electron** around the **nucleus** of an **atom.**

orbital Region around the **nucleus** of an **atom** in which there is high probability of finding an **electron**. *See* **atomic orbital**; **molecular orbital**.

orbital electron Electron that **orbits** the **nucleus** of an **atom.** Alternative name: planetary electron.

oscillation Regular variation in position or state about a mean value.

oscillator Device or electronic circuit for producing an **alternating current** of a particular frequency, usually controlled by altering the value of a **capacitor** in the oscillator circuit.

oscilloscope *See* **cathode-ray oscilloscope.**

osmosis Movement of a solvent from a dilute to a more concentrated solution across a **semipermeable** (or differentially permeable) **membrane**.

osmotic pressure Pressure required to stop **osmosis** between a solution and pure water.

output device Part of a **computer** that presents **data** in a form that can be used by a human operator; *e.g.*, a **printer, visual display unit (VDU),** chart plotter, etc. A machine that writes **data** onto a portable magnetic medium (*e.g.*, magnetic disk or tape) may also be considered to be an output device.

overtone Harmonic; a note of higher frequency than a fundamental note.

P

packing fraction Difference between the actual mass of an **isotope** and the nearest whole number divided by the **mass number**.

paper tape *See* **punched tape**.

parallax Apparent change in the position of an object when it is observed from two different viewpoints.

parallel Alternative name for **latitude**.

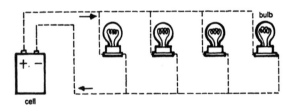

Four lamps connected in parallel

parallel circuit Electrical circuit in which the voltage supply is connected to each side of all the components so that only a fraction of the total current flows through each of them. For **capacitors** in parallel, the total capacitance C is equal to the sum of the individual capacitances; *i.e.*, $C = C_1 + C_2 + C_3 + ...$ For **resistors** in parallel, the reciprocal of the total resistance R is equal to the sum of the reciprocals of the individual resistances; *i.e.*, $1/R = 1/R_1 + 1/R_2 + 1/R_3 ...$

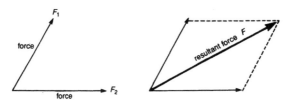

Parallelogram of forces gives the resultant

parallelogram of forces Method of finding a resultant of two forces by using the **parallelogram of vectors**.

parallelogram of vectors Method of finding the single resultant of two vectors by drawing them to scale, separated by the correct angle, and completing the parallelogram of which they are two sides. The diagonal of the parallelogram from that angle represents the magnitude and direction of the resultant vector.

paramagnetism Property of substances that posses a small permanent **magnetic moment** because of the presence of odd (unpaired) **electrons**; the substance becomes magnetized in a magnetic field as the magnetic moments align.

parsec Unit of astronomical distance equivalent to 3.26 **light-years** (3.086×10^{13} km). At that distance, a length of 1 astronomical unit subtends an angle of 1 second of arc.

partial pressure *See* **Dalton's law of partial pressures**.

particle Minute portion of matter, often taken to mean an **atom, molecule** or **elementary particle** or **subatomic particle**.

particle accelerator Machine for producing a beam of high-speed **particles,** such as those that are used to disintegrate atomic nuclei.

particle physics Branch of science concerned with the properties of **elementary particles**.

partition coefficient Ratio of the concentrations of a single **solute** in two immiscible **solvents**, at equilibrium. It is independent of the actual concentrations.

pascal (Pa) SI unit of pressure, equal to a force of 1 newton per square meter ($N\ m^{-2}$). It was named after the French physicist and mathematician Blaise Pascal (1623–1662).

Pascal's law In a fluid, the pressure applied at any point is transmitted equally throughout it. It is the principle by which hydraulic machinery works.

Pauli exclusion principle No two **electrons** can be assigned the same set of **quantum numbers,** hence there can be only two electrons in any one atomic **orbital**. It was named after the Austrian-born American physicist Wolfgang Pauli (1900–1958). Alternative name: exclusion principle.

PD Abbreviation of **potential difference**.

pendulum A simple pendulum consists of a weight (called a bob) at the end of a string that over small angles, swings with **simple harmonic motion**. The period of swing t is given by $t = 2\pi(l/g)^{1/2}$, where l is the length of the string and g is the acceleration of free fall. *See also* **compound pendulum**.

period (t) Time taken to complete a regular cycle, such as a complete swing of a pendulum or one cycle of any type of simple harmonic motion.

periodic function Function that returns to the same value at regular intervals.

peripheral unit Equipment that can be linked to a **computer,** including input, output and storage devices.

periscope Device for viewing objects that are above eye level, or placed so that direct vision is obstructed. Light rays entering the top of a tube pass into a right-angled prism, which reflects them straight downward to the bottom of the tube, where a second prism reflects into the eye of the viewer. Angled mirrors may replace the prisms in a simple periscope.

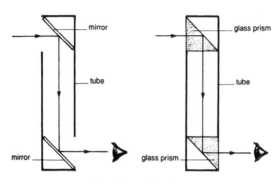

Two types of periscopes

permanent magnet Ferromagnetic objects that retains a permanent **magnetic field** and the **magnetic moment** associated with it after the magnetizing field has been removed.

permeability 1. Rate at which a substance diffuses through a porous material. 2. Magnetization developed in a material placed in a magnetic field, equal to the **flux density** produced divided by the **magnetic field strength.** Alternative name: magnetic permeability.

permittivity, absolute (ϵ) For a material placed in an **electric field**, the ratio of the electric displacement to the electric field strength producing it.

permittivity, relative For a material placed in an **electric field**, the ratio of the electric displacement to that which would be produced in free space by the same field. Alternative names: dielectric constant, inductivity, specific capacitance.

personal computer (PC) *See* **microcomputer**.

perturbation theory Method of obtaining approximate solutions to equations representing the behavior of a system. It is used in **quantum mechanics**.

phase 1. Any homogeneous and physically distinct part of a (chemical) system that is separated from other parts of the system by definite boundaries, *e.g.*, ice mixed with water. 2. The part of a periodically varying waveform that has been completed at a particular moment.

phase contrast microscope Microscope that uses the principle that light passing through materials of different **refractive indices** undergoes a change in phase, transmitting these changes as different intensities of light given off by different materials.

phase rule The number of **degrees of freedom** (*F*) of a **heterogeneous** system is related to the number of components (*C*) and of phases (*P*) present at **equilibrium** by the equation $P + F = C + 2$.

phosphor Substance capable of **luminescence** or **phosphorescence**, as used to coat the inside of a television screen or fluorescent lamp.

phosphorescence Emission of light (generally visible light) after **absorption** of light of another wavelength (usually ultraviolet or near ultraviolet) or electrons; unlike **fluorescence,** it continues after the stimulating source is removed. See also: **luminescence.**

photocell Device that converts light into an electric current. It can be used for the detection and measurement of light intensity. Alternative names: photoelectric cell, photoemissive cell, photovoltaic cell.

photochromism Change in color of a substance through exposure to light; *e.g.*, photochromic glass, used in sunglasses.

photoconductivity Change in electrical conductivity of a substance when it is exposed to light; *e.g.*, selenium, used in photoelectric light meters. *See also* **light-dependent resistor.**

photoelectric cell Alternative name for **photocell**.

photoelectric effect Phenomenon that occurs with some semi-metallic materials. When **photons** strike them they are absorbed and the energized **electrons** produced flow in the material as an electric current. It is the basis of photocells and instruments that employ them, such as photographers' light meters and burglar alarms.

photoelectron Electron produced by the **photoelectric effect** or by **photoionization**.

photoemission Emission of **photoelectrons** by the **photoelectric effect** or by **photoionization**.

photography Process of taking photographs by the chemical action of light or other radiation on a sensitive plate or film made of glass, celluloid or other transparent material coated with a light-sensitive emulsion. Light causes changes in particles of silver salts in the emulsion that, after development (in a reducing agent), form grains of dark metallic silver to produce a negative image. Unaffected silver salts are removed by fixing (in a solution of ammonium or sodium thiosulphate).

photoionization Ionization of atoms or molecules by light or other **electromagnetic radiation**.

photoluminescence Light emission by a substance after it has itself been exposed to visible light or infrared or ultraviolet radiation.

photometer Instrument for measuring the intensity of light.

photometry Measurement of the intensity of light.

photomicrograph Photograph obtained through a microscope.

photomultiplier Photocell of high sensitivity used for detecting very small quantities of light radiation. It consists of series of electrodes in an evacuated envelope, which are used to amplify the emission current by electron multiplication. Alternative name: electron multiplier.

photon

photon **Quantum** of **electromagnetic radiation**, such as light or X-rays; a "packet" of radiation. The amount of energy per photon is *hn*, where *h* is **Planck's constant** and *n* is the frequency of the radiation.

photoneutron **Neutron** resulting from the interaction of a **photon** with an atomic **nucleus**.

photovoltaic cell Alternative name for a **photocell**.

physical change Reversible alteration in the properties of a substance that does not affect the composition of the substance itself (as opposed to a chemical change, which is difficult to reverse and in which composition is affected).

physical states of matter Three kinds of substances that make up matter: gases, liquids and solids.

physics Science concerned with the properties of matter, energy and radiation, particularly in processes involving no change of chemical composition.

piezoelectric effect Production of a measurable electric current by some crystals when they are subjected to mechanical compression. It is widely exploited in gramophone pick-ups and some types of **microphones**. The effect is also exploited in reverse, with an electrical current producing physical distortion, *e.g.*, in some loudspeakers, gas-fueled cigarette lighters and quartz (crystal) watches and clocks.

Pitot tube Device for measuring the speed of a moving fluid consisting of an open-ended cylindrical tube pointing into the flow. The other end of the tube has a hole at the side. The difference in pressure between the dynamic pressure at the open end and the static pressure at the side is a measure of the speed of fluid flow (*e.g.*, as displayed by an air-speed indicator). It was named after the French physicist Henri Pitot (1695–1771).

Planck's constant (*h*) Fundamental constant that relates the energy of a **quantum** of **radiation** to the frequency of the oscillator that emits it. The relationship is $E = hv$, where E is the energy of the quantum and v is its frequency. Its value is 6.626196×10^{-34} joule second. It was named after the German physicist Max Planck (1858–1947).

Planck's radiation law An object cannot emit or absorb energy, in the form of radiation, in a continuous manner; the energy can be taken up or given out only as integral multiples of a definite amount, known as a **quantum**. Alternative name: Planck's law of radiation.

planetary electron Alternative name for **orbital electron.**

plasma State of matter in which the atoms or molecules of a substance are broken into **electrons** and positive **ions.** All substances pass into this state of matter when heated to a very high temperature, *e.g.*, in an electric arc or in the interior of a star.

pneumatic Operated by air pressure.

polarization 1. Lining up of the electric and magnetic fields of an **electromagnetic wave**, *e.g.*, as in **polarized light**. Only transverse waves can be polarized. 2. Formation of gas bubbles or a film of deposit on an electrode of an **electrolytic cell,** which tends to impede the flow of current.

polarized light Light waves (which normally oscillate in all possible planes) with fixed orientation of the electric and magnetic fields. It may be created by passing the light through a polarizer consisting of a plate of tourmaline crystal cut in a special way, by using a **Polaroid** sheet.

Polaroid Trade name for a thin, transparent film that produces plane-**polarized light** when light is passed through it.

pole 1. North or south end of Earth's axis. 2. **Magnetic pole.** 3. **Electrode** (particularly of a battery).

polymorphism Occurrence of a substance in more than one crystalline form.

population inversion Condition in which a higher energy state in an atomic system is more populated with electrons than a lower energy state.

porosity Property of substance that allows gases or liquids to pass through it.

positive 1. Describing an **electric charge** or **ion** that is attracted by a negative one. 2. Describing a north-seeking **magnetic pole**.

positive feedback Feedback in which the output adds to the input.

positron Elementary particle that has a mass equal to that of an **electron**, and an electrical charge equal in magnitude, but opposite in sign, to that of the electron.

potential difference (PD) Difference in electric potential between two points in a current-carrying circuit, usually expressed in volts (V). Alternative name: voltage.

potential energy Energy possessed by an object because of its position, or because it is stretched or compressed (*e.g.*, a spring). For instance, because of its position a mass m at a height h has potential energy mgh (where g is the acceleration of free fall). *See also* **kinetic energy**.

potentiometer 1. Instrument for measuring **potential difference** or **electromotive force**. 2. **Voltage divider**.

pound Unit of weight, abbreviation lb, equal to 16 ounces; 14 lb = 1 stone, 112 lb = 1 hundredweight (cwt). 1 lb = 0.4536 kg.

power 1. In physics, rate of doing **work**. The SI unit of power is the **watt** (equal to 10^7 erg s^{-1} or 1/745.7 horsepower). 2. In optics, the extent to which a curved mirror, lens or optical instrument can magnify an object. For a simple lens, power is expressed in **diopters**.

pressure (p) Force applied to, or distributed over, a surface; measured as force f per unit area a; $p = f / a$. At a depth d in a liquid, the pressure is given by $p = \rho gd$, where ρ is the liquid's density and g is the acceleration of free fall. The SI unit of pressure is the **pascal**; other units include bars, millibars, atmospheres and millimeters of mercury (mm Hg). *See also* **atmospheric pressure.**

pressure gauge Device for measuring fluid **pressure** (*e.g.*, barometer, manometer).

pressurized water reactor (PWR) **Nuclear reactor** in which the heat generated in the nuclear core is removed by water (reactor coolant), circulating at high pressure to prevent it from boiling.

primary cell Electrolytic cell (battery) in which the chemical reactions that cause the current flow are not readily reversible and the cell cannot easily be recharged, *e.g.*, a **dry cell.** *See also* **secondary cell.**

primary color 1. Red, green and violet, which give all other colors when light producing them is combined in various proportions. All three mix to give white. 2. Pigment colors red, yellow and blue, which can also be combined to give pigments of all other colors. All three mix to give black.

printer Computer **output device** that produces **hard copy** as a printout. There are various kinds, including (in order of speed) daisy-wheel, dot-matrix, line, barrel and laser.

printout Output (**hard copy**) from a computer **printer.**

prism, optical Transparent solid with triangular ends and rectangular sides, with refracting surfaces at acute angles with each other.

probability distribution of electrons Probability that an **electron** within an atom will be at a certain point in space at a given time. It predicts the shape of an atomic **orbital.**

program Sequence of instructions for a computer.

projectile Object that is projected or thrown by force, often referring to a bullet or shell fired from a gun.

propagation Directional transmission of energy in the form of waves, *e.g.*, sound, radio waves.

proton Fundamental **elementary particle** with a positive charge equal in magnitude to the negative charge on an **electron**, and with a mass about 1,850 times that of an electron. Protons are constituents of the **nucleus** in every kind of **atom.**

proton number Alternative name for **atomic number.**

psi particle Meson that has no charge, but a very long lifetime. Alternative name: J-particle.

***p*-type conductivity** Conductivity that results from the movement of positive holes (**lattice** sites of a crystalline **semiconductor** that are occupied by an acceptor impurity atom—*i.e.*, an atom with one fewer valence electrons than the semiconductor).

***p*-type semiconductor** Form of **semiconductor** that exhibits *p*-type conductivity.

pulley Simple machine that changes the direction of an applied force or, if it uses more than one pulley wheel, provides a **mechanical advantage** (force ratio) equal to the ratio of the resultant pulling force to the applied force.

pulse In physics and telecommunications, brief disturbance propagated in a similar way as a **wave**, but not having the continuous periodic nature of a wave.

pump Mechanical device for transferring liquids or gases, or for compressing gases. A simple lift pump employs atmospheric pressure and cannot pump a liquid vertically more than about 10 m (32 feet); a force pump does not have this restriction.

punched card Computer input or output medium consisting of cards punched with coded holes. The actual input device is a punched card reader; the output device is a card punch.

punched tape Computer input of output medium consisting of paper tape punched with coded holes. The actual input device is a punched tape reader; the output device is a tape punch.

pyroelectricity Polarization of certain **crystals** by the application of heat.

pyrometer Instrument for measuring high temperatures, above the range of liquid thermometers.

pyrometry Measurement of high temperatures.

Q

quanta Plural of **quantum.**

quantum Unit quantity (an indivisible "packet") of energy postulated in the **quantum theory.** The **photon** is the quantum of **electromagnetic radiation** (such as light) and in certain contexts the **meson** is the quantum of the nuclear field.

quantum electrodynamics Study of **electromagnetic interactions,** in accordance with the **quantum theory.**

quantum electronics Generation or amplification of **microwave** power, governed by **quantum mechanics.**

quantum mechanics Method of dealing with the behavior of small particles such as **electrons** and **nuclei.** It uses the idea of the particle-wave duality of matter. Thus an electron has a dual nature, particle and wave, but it behaves as one or the other according to the nature of the experiment.

quantum number Integer or half-integral number that specifies possible values of a quantitized physical quantity, *e.g.*, energy level, nuclear spin, angular momentum, etc.

quantum state State of an **atom, electron, particle**, etc., defined by a unique set of **quantum numbers.**

quantum theory Theory of radiation. It states that radiant energy is given out by a radiating body in separate units of energy known as **quanta**; the same applies to the absorption of radiation. The total amount of radiant energy given out or absorbed is always a whole number of quanta.

quark Subatomic particle that combines with others to form a **hadron**. Current theory predicts six types of quarks and six antiquarks, but none has yet been observed.

R

racemic mixture Optically inactive mixture that contains equal amounts of **dextrorotatory** and **levorotatory** forms of an **optically active** compound.

racemization Transformation of **optically active** compounds into **racemic mixtures**. It can be affected by the action of heat or light, or by the use of chemical reagents.

rad Unit of absorbed dose of ionizing **radiation**, equivalent to 100 ergs per gram (0.01 J kg^{-1}) of absorbing material. The corresponding SI unit is the gray.

radar Abbreviation of radio detection and ranging, a method of detecting objects, and their bearing and distance, by transmitting continuous or pulsed radio waves and receiving their echos.

radian (rad) SI unit of plane angle; the angle at the center of a circle subtended by an arc whose length is equal to the radius of the circle. 1 radian = 57 degrees (approx.).

radiance **Radiant flux** per unit area of a surface.

radiant Describing something that emits **electromagnetic radiation** (*e.g.*, light, heat rays).

radiant flux The rate at which **power** is emitted or received by an object in the form of **electromagnetic radiation**.

radiant heat Heat that is transmitted in the form of **infrared radiation**.

radiation Energy that travels in the form of **electromagnetic radiation**, *e.g.*, **radio waves**, **infrared radiation**, **light**, **ultraviolet radiation**, **X-rays** and **gamma rays**. The term is also applied to the rays of **alpha** and **beta particles** emitted by **radioactive** substances. Particle rays and short-wavelength electromagnetic radiation may be harmful to tissues because they are **ionizing radiation.**

radiation pressure Minute force exerted on a surface by **electromagnetic radiation** that strikes it.

radiation unit Activity of a **radio-isotope** expressed in units of disintegrations per second, called the **becquerel** in SI units. Formerly it was measured in **curies.**

radiator 1. Object that emits **radiation.** 2. Heat exchanger that is used either to dissipate the heat from a coolant fluid (*e.g.*, car radiator) or emit heat from a hot fluid (*e.g.*, space heater for buildings).

radio Method of telecommunications that uses **radio waves.** The transmitted signal modulates the **amplitude** (AM) or **frequency** (FM) of a carrier wave, which is picked up by an **aerial** (antenna) at the receiver, which demodulates it and usually drives a **loudspeaker.**

radioactive Possessing or exhibiting **radioactivity.**

radioactive decay Way in which a **radioactive** element spontaneously changes into another element or **isotope** by the emission of **alpha** or **beta particles** or **gamma rays.** The rate at which it does so is represented by its **half-life.**

radioactive equilibrium Condition attained when a parent **radioactive** element produces a daughter radioactive element that decays at the same rate as it is being formed from the parent.

radioactive standard Radio-isotope of known rate of **radioactive decay** used for the calibration of **radiation**-measuring instruments.

radioactive tracing Use of **radio-isotopes** to study the movement and behavior of an element through a biological or chemical system by observing the intensity of its **radioactivity.**

radioactive waste Hazardous **radio-isotopes** (fission products) that accumulate as waste products in a **nuclear reactor**. They have to be periodically removed and stored safely or reprocessed. The term is also applied to the waste ("tailings") produced by the processing of uranium ores.

radioactivity Spontaneous disintegration of atomic **nuclei**, usually with the emission of **alpha particles**, **beta particles** or **gamma rays.**

radio frequency (RF) Frequency of **electromagnetic radiation** suitable for **radio** transmission, *i.e.*, from about 10 kHz to 300,000 MHz.

radiograph Photographic image that results from uneven absorption by an object being subjected to penetrating radiation. An X-ray photograph is a common example.

radiography Photography using **X-rays** or **gamma rays**, particularly in medical applications.

radio-isotope Isotope that emits **radioactivity** (ionizing radiation) during its spontaneous decay. Radio-isotopes are useful sources of radiation (*e.g.*, in **radiography**) and are used as tracers for **radioactive tracing.**

radiology Study of **X-rays, gamma rays** and **radioactivity** (including **radio-isotopes**), especially as used in diagnosis and treatment.

radioluminescence Fluorescence caused by **radioactivity**.

radio-opaque Resistant to the penetrating effects of radiation, especially **X-rays**; the term is often used to describe substances injected into the body before a **radiography** examination.

radio telescope Telescope, used in astronomy, that can pick up radio signals from extraterrestrial sources. It produces electrical signals that are often recorded graphically.

radio wave Form of high-frequency **electromagnetic radiation** with a **wavelength** greater than a few millimeters.

radius of curvature Of a point on a curve, the radius of a circle that touches the inside of the curve at that point.

radius of gyration Of a rotating object, the distance from the axis of rotation at which the total mass of the object might be concentrated without changing its **moment of inertia**.

radius vector For a point in a plane with the polar coordinates (r, θ), the distance from the origin to the point, equal to r.

rainbow Arc of spectral colors, seen in the sky opposite the sun from certain angles only, that results from the reflection and refraction of sunlight by raindrops.

RAM Abbreviation of **random access memory** of a **computer**.

r.a.m Abbreviation of **relative atomic mass** (formerly called atomic weight).

Raman effect Scattering of **monochromatic light**, when it passes through a transparent homogeneous medium, into different **wavelengths** because of interaction with the molecules of the medium.

random access memory (RAM) Part of a computer's **memory** that can be written to and read from. *See also* **ROM**.

Rankine scale Temperature scale that expresses **absolute temperatures** in degrees Fahrenheit (absolute zero = 0°R). It was named after the British engineer and physicist William Rankine (1820–1872).

Raoult's law The relative lowering of the **vapor pressure** of a **solution** is proportional to the **mole** fraction of the **solute** in the solution at a particular temperature. It was named after the French scientist Francois Raoult (1830–1901).

raster Display of information in the form of a grid, usually referring to the image produced by the scanning action of a **cathode-ray tube**, *e.g.*, in a television receiver.

ray Beam of any type of radiation (*e.g.*, light, cathode rays). In ray diagrams showing the behavior of mirrors and lenses, rays of light are drawn as straight lines.

reactance (X) Property of a **capacitance** or **inductance** in a circuit carrying alternating current (a.c.) that makes it oppose the passage of current; the imaginary part of **impedance**. It is measured in ohms. For a pure capacitance C, $X = \frac{1}{2}\pi fC$, where f is the frequency of the a.c.; for a pure inductance L, $X = 2\pi fL$.

reactor Alternative name for a **nuclear reactor.**

read head Electromagnetic device on a tape recorder, video recorder or computer that "reads" signals stored on a magnetic tape, disk or drum.

read-only memory (ROM) Part of a computer's **memory** that can only be read (and not written to). *See also* **random access memory.**

read-write head Electromagnetic device that functions as both a **read head** and a **write head**.

reciprocal wavelength Alternative name for **wave number.**

record In computing, a number of elements of data that together form one unit of stored information.

rectification Conversion of **alternating current** (a.c.) into **direct current** (d.c.) using a **rectifier.**

rectifier Electrical device, such as a **diode**, for converting an **alternating current** (a.c.) into a **direct current** (d.c.). It may take the form of a plate rectifier, a **diode** valve or a **semiconductor** diode.

reduced equation of state

reduced equation of state Law stating that if any two or more substances have the same reduced pressure π—*i.e.*, their pressures are the same fraction or multiple π of their respective **critical pressures**—and are at equal reduced temperatures θ then their reduced volumes φ should be equal.

reduced pressure distillation Alternative name for **vacuum distillation**.

reduced temperature, pressure and volume Quantities θ, π and φ that are the ratios of the temperature, pressure and volume to the **critical temperature**, **critical pressure** and **critical volume** respectively in the **reduced equation of state**.

reflectance Ratio of the intensity of reflected **radiation** to the intensity of the incident radiation.

reflecting telescope Astronomical **telescope** that uses mirrors to produce an enlarged image. By multiple reflection, mirrors can "fold" the light path, so making the telescope shorter than one using only lenses; also mirrors are lighter, and can be made larger, than glass lenses of comparable power. Alternative name: reflector.

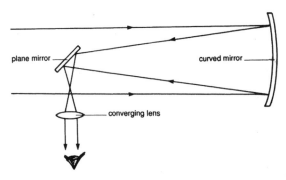

A Newtonian reflecting telescope

reflection, angle of Angle between a reflected ray of light and the normal.

reflection of light Change in direction of a light ray after it strikes a polished surface (*e.g.*, a mirror).

reflection of light, laws of 1. The angle of reflection equals the angle or incidence. 2. The reflected ray is in the same plane as the incident ray and the normal at the point of incidence.

reflector 1. Object or surface that reflects **electromagnetic radiation** (*e.g.*, light, radio waves), particularly one around or inside a lamp to concentrate a light beam. 2. Alternative name for **reflecting telescope**.

refracting telescope Astronomical **telescope** that has two converging lenses, one an objective of long focal length and the other an eyepiece of short focal length. Alternative name: refractor.

refraction, angle of Angle between a refracted ray of light and the normal.

refraction correction Small correction that has to be made to the observed altitude of a heavenly body because of the **refraction of light** by Earth's atmosphere. All bodies appear to be higher than they actually are.

refraction of light Change in direction of a light ray as it passes obliquely from one transparent medium to another of different **refractive index.**

refraction of light, laws of 1. For two particular media, the ratio of the sine of the angle of incidence to the sine of the angle of refraction is constant (the **refractive index**). This is a statement of Snell's law. 2. The refracted ray is in the same plane as the incident ray and the normal at the point of incidence.

refractive constant Alternative name for **refractive index.**

refractive index μ Ratio of the speed of **electromagnetic radiation** (such as light) in air or vacuum to its speed in another medium. The speed depends on the **wavelength** of the radiation as well as on the **density** of the medium. For a

refractometer

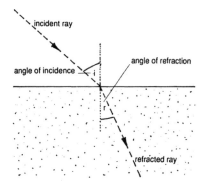

Refraction of light between two media

refracted ray of light, it is equal to the ratio of the sine of the angle of incidence i to the sine of the angle or refraction r; *i.e.*, $\mu = \sin i / \sin r$. Alternative name: refractive constant.

refractometer Instrument for measuring the **refractive index** of a substance.

refractor Alternative name for **refracting telescope**.

regelation Refreezing of ice that has been melted by pressure when the pressure is removed.

relative atomic mass (r.a.m.) Mass of an atom relative to the mass of the isotope carbon-12 (which is taken to be exactly 12). Former name: atomic weight.

relative density Ratio of the **density** of a given substance to the density of some reference substance. For liquids, relative densities are usually expressed with reference to the density of water at 4°C. Former name: specific gravity.

relative humidity Ratio of the **pressure** of water vapor present in air to the pressure the water vapor would have if the air were saturated at the same temperature (*i.e.*, to the saturated water vapor pressure). It is expressed as a percentage.

relative molecular mass Sum of the **relative atomic masses** of all the atoms in a molecule of a substance. Alternative name: molecular weight.

relative permeability For a material placed in a **magnetic field,** the ratio of its **permeability** to the permeability of free space.

relativity Einstein's theory; scientific principle expressing in mathematical and physical terms the implications of the fact that observations depend as much on the viewpoint as on what is being observed.

relay, electrical Electric switching device that brings about changes in an independent circuit.

reluctance Total **magnetic flux** in a magnetic circuit when a **magnetomotive force** is applied.

reluctivity Reciprocal of magnetic **permeability**. Alternative name: specific reluctance.

rem Abbreviation of röntgen equivalent man, the quantity of **ionizing radiation** such that the energy imparted to a biological system per gram of living material has the same effect as one **röntgen**.

resistance, electrical Property of an electrical **conductor** that makes it oppose the flow of **current** through it. It is measured in **ohms**.

resistivity Property of a material that makes it oppose the flow of an electric current. For a given specimen of a conductor, it is the product of its resistance R and cross-sectional area A divided by its length l, at a specified temperature (in units of ohm meters). Alternative name: specific resistance.

resistor Device that provides **resistance** in electrical circuits.

resolution of forces Process of division of **forces** into components that act in specified directions. *See also* **resultant**.

resonance

resonance 1. Movement of **electrons** from one **atom** of a **molecule** or **ion** to another atom of that molecule or ion. **2.** Phenomenon in which a system is made to vibrate at its natural frequency as a result of vibrations received from another source of the same frequency.

restitution, coefficient of Ratio of the difference in velocity of two colliding objects after impact to the difference before impact. An elastic object that bounces well has a high coefficient of restitution.

resultant Of two or more **vectors**, the single vector that has the same effect. It can be found by constructing the **parallelogram of vectors**.

Reynolds number (Re) Dimensionless quantity of the form $LV \rho/\mu$ that is proportional to the ratio of inertial force to viscous force in a liquid flowing through a cylindrical tube, where L is diameter of the tube, V is linear velocity, ρ is fluid density and μ is fluid viscosity. The critical Reynolds number corresponds to the change from turbulent flow to laminar flow as the velocity is reduced.

rheostat Variable resistor, used to control voltage (*e.g.*, as the volume control in audio equipment).

right-hand rule 1. Rule that relates the direction of induced current, magnetic field and movements in electromagnetic induction. If the right hand is held with the thumb, first and second fingers at right angles, the thumb represents the direction of movement, the first finger the direction of the magnetic field and the second finger the direction of the induced current. Alternative name: Fleming's right-hand rule (*see* **left-hand rule**). **2.** Rule that gives the direction of the concentric magnetic field around a current-carrying conductor. If the right hand is held with the thumb directed upward to represent the direction of the current, the fingers curl around in the direction of the magnetic field. Alternative name: right-hand grip rule.

rigidity modulus Measure of the resistance of an object or material to a shearing **strain**, equal to the shear force per unit area divided by the angular deformation. Alternative name: shear modulus.

ring main Method of wiring electric power sockets so that they are concerned in **parallel** to a supply that forms a ring or chain (typically around one floor of a building), instead of wiring each socket back to a single supply point.

ripple tank Apparatus for demonstrating the behavior of water waves, which in many cases is analogous to the behavior of other types of wave motion.

roentgen Alternative name for **röntgen**.

ROM Abbreviation of **read-only memory** of a **computer**.

röntgen (R) Unit of radiation; the amount of **X-rays** or **gamma rays** that produce a charge of 2.58×10^{-4} coulomb of electricity in 1 cm^3 of dry air. Alternative name: roentgen.

röntgen rays Alternative name for **X-rays**.

rotary converter Electric motor combined with a **dynamo**, used to convert an **alternating current** (a.c.) to a **direct current** (d.c.).

rotatory Optically active; capable of rotating the plane of **polarized light**.

rotoscope Alternative name for **stroboscope**.

Rydberg constant (R) Constant relating to the **wave number** of atomic spectrum lines. Its value for hydrogen is 1.09677×10^7 m^{-1}. It was named after the Swedish physicist Johannes Rydberg (1854–1919).

Rydberg formula Formula for expressing the **wave number** of a spectral line. The general Rydberg formula is given by the equation $1/\lambda = R(1/n^2 - 1/m^2)$, where n and m are positive integers, and R is the **Rydberg constant**.

S

salt bridge Tube that contains a saturated solution of potassium chloride, or an agar gel made with concentrated potassium chloride solution. It is employed to connect two **half-cells**.

saturated solution Solution that cannot take up any more **solute** at a given temperature. *See also* **supersaturated solution**.

saturated vapor Vapor that can exist in **equilibrium** with its parent **solid** or **liquid** at a given temperature.

saturated vapor pressure Pressure exerted by a **saturated vapor**. It is temperature dependent.

saturation Point at which no more of a material can be dissolved, absorbed or retained by another.

sawtooth wave Electronically generated waveform (typically a voltage varying with time) that has a uniform increase of the variable that drops rapidly to the initial value at regular intervals. It is used, *e.g.*, as a **time base** for scanning circuits for a **cathode-ray tube**.

scalar Quantity that has magnitude but not direction (unlike a **vector**, which has both).

scaler Electronic device whose circuits measuring the amount of charge or energy transfer resulting from radiation. *See also* **counter**.

scanning electron microscope Electron microscope that scans the sample to be examined with a beam of **electrons**.

scattering of light Irregular reflection or diffraction of light rays that occurs when a beam of light passes through a material medium.

Schrödinger equation Equation that treats the behavior of an **electron** in an **atom** as a three-dimensional **stationary wave**. Its solution is related to the probability that the electron is located in a particular place. It was named after the Austrian physicist Erwin Schrödinger (1887–1961). Alternative name: Schrödinger wave equation.

scintillation counter Device that counts the incidence of **photons** upon a material by the visible or near-visible light that is emitted.

scintillation spectrometer **Scintillation counter** capable of measuring the energy and the intensity of **gamma radiation** emitted from a material.

second 1. SI unit of time, defined as the duration of 9,192,631,770 periods of the **radiation** between the two hyperfine levels of the ground state of the cesium-139 atom. Abbreviated to sec or s. 2. Angle equal to $\frac{1}{60}$ of a minute or $\frac{1}{360}$ of a degree.

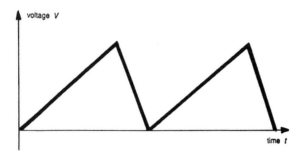

Simple sawtooth wave

secondary cell **Electrolytic cell** that must be supplied with **electric charge** before use by passing a direct current through it, but it can be recharged over and over again. Alternative names: accumulator, storage cell. *See also* **primary cell**.

secondary color Color obtained by mixing **primary colors**.

self-absorption Decrease in **radiation** from a large **radioactive** source due to **absorption** by the material itself of some of the radiation produced. Alternative name: self-shielding.

self-induced electromotive force Production of an **electromotive force** (e.m.f.) in an electric circuit when the current is varied.

self-induction Resistance to a change in **current** in an electric circuit by the creation of a back **electromotive force**.

semiconductor Substance that is an **insulator** at very low temperatures but which becomes a **conductor** if the temperature is raised or when it is slightly impure. Semiconductors are used in **rectifiers** and photoelectric devices, and for making **diodes** and **transistors**. *See also* **donor; doping; *n*-type conductivity; *p*-type conductivity**.

semipermeable membrane Porous **membrane** that permits the passage of some substances but not others; *e.g.*, plasma membrane, which permits entry of small molecules such as water but not large molecules, allowing **osmosis** to occur. Such membranes are extremely important in biological systems and are used in **dialysis**. Alternative name: selectively permeable membrane.

series Describing the arrangement of components in a **series circuit**.

series circuit Electrical circuit in which the components are arranged one after the other so that the same current flows through each of them. For a series of **resistors**, the total resistance R is equal to the sum of the individual resistances; *i.e.*, $R = R_1 + R_2 + R_3 \ldots$ For a series of **capacitors**, the reciprocal of the total capacitance C is equal to the sum of the reciprocals of the individual capacitances; *i.e.*, $1/C = 1/C_1 + 1/C_2 + 1/C_3 \ldots$

servomechanism Device that uses a small amount of power to control the activity of a much more powerful device (*e.g.*, as in power-assisted steering on a motor vehicle).

shear Deformation in which parallel planes in a material slide over each other (but remain parallel).

shear modulus Alternative name for **rigidity modulus**.

shear stress **Shear** force per unit cross-sectional area.

shell In atomic physics, group of **electrons** that share the same principal **quantum number** in an atom. The particles that form an atomic nucleus are also thought to occupy shells.

shock wave **Sound** wave in air, of exceptionally high intensity, produced by an object traveling faster than the **speed of sound** or by the detonation of a high explosive.

short circuit Electric circuit through a very low **resistance**, which passes a very high current, usually caused accidentally when insulation fails.

shunt In physics, resistor connected in series with a circuit or device (*e.g.*, a meter) that reduces the amount of electric current flowing through it. *See also* **multiplier**.

silicon chip **Integrated circuit** made from a thin wafer of pure crystalline silicon. Alternating insulating and **semiconductor** layers are printed on the wafer. The pattern of an electronic control circuit is also etched onto it.

simple harmonic motion Periodic motion of a particle whose **acceleration** (a) is proportional to its distance (x) from a fixed point and is always directed toward that point; *i.e.*, $a = -kx$, where k is a constant. The minus sign shows that, as the particle moves to and fro, its acceleration is oppositely directed to its displacement.

simple pendulum *See* **pendulum**.

sine wave Waveform that represents the periodic oscillations of constant **amplitude** as given by the sine of a linear function. Alternative names: sinusoidal wave, sine curve.

siphon Device consisting of an inverted U-shaped tube that moves a liquid from one place to another place at a lower level. The tube has to be filled with liquid before being put into position.

SI units Abbreviation for Systéme International d'Unités, an international system of scientific units. It has seven basic units: **meter** (m), **kilogram** (kg), **second** (s), **kelvin** (K), **ampere** (A), **mole** (mol) and **candela** (cd), and two supplementary units: **radian** (rad) and **steradian** (sr). There are also 18 derived units.

slow neutron Alternative name for **thermal neutron**.

soft iron Iron that has a low content of carbon, unlike steel. It is unable to retain **magnetism**.

soft radiation Radiation of relatively long **wavelength** whose penetrating power is very limited.

software Program that can be used on a **computer**; *e.g.,* executive programs, operating systems and utility programs. *See also* **hardware**.

solar cell Photocell that converts **solar energy** directly into **electricity**.

solar energy Energy from the sun, mainly light and heat radiation. It can be harnessed to make electricity using **photocells**, or the sun's rays may be used directly to heat water in a radiator or, focused by mirrors, in a solar furnace. Solar energy also provides the energy for photosynthesis, which is an essential process for the existence of life on Earth.

solar heating Heating from a domestic or industrial heater that uses solar energy, generally to heat water.

solar wind Continuous permanent stream of electrically charged particles that are emitted from the sun.

solenoid Cylindrical coil of wire, carrying an electric current, used to produce a **magnetic field**. It may have an iron core that moves, often to work a switch. *See also* **relay**.

solid 1. Object having the three dimensions of length, breadth and thickness; a solid figure. 2. Alternative name for a substance in the **solid state**.

solidifying point Alternative name for **freezing point**.

solid solution Single solid **homogeneous** crystalline **phase** of two or more substances. Many alloys are solid solutions.

solid state Physical **state of matter** that has a definite shape and resists having it changed; the volume of a solid changes only slightly with **temperature** and **pressure**. A true solid state is associated with a definite **crystalline** form, although **amorphous** solids also exist (*e.g.*, glass). Alternative name: solid.

solid-state physics Branch of **physics** concerned with matter in the **solid state**, particularly **semiconductors** and **superconductors**.

solubility Amount of a substance (**solute**) that will dissolve in a liquid (**solvent**) at a given temperature, usually expressed as a mass per unit volume (*e.g.*, gm per liter) or a percentage.

solute Substance that dissolves in a **solvent** to form a **solution**.

solution Homogeneous mixture of **solute** and **solvent**.

solvent Substance in which a **solute** dissolves; the component of a **solution** that is in excess.

sonar Abbreviation of sound navigation and ranging, an apparatus for echo sounding that employs **ultrasonic** waves. It can detect echoes from underwater objects and so give their bearing and range. Alternative name: underwater **radar**.

sonometer Apparatus for investigating stretched wires or strings as sources of sound.

Soret effect *See* **thermal diffusion**.

sound Periodic vibrations that travel as pressure waves through media and to which the ears of human beings and other animals may be sensitive. There must be a medium; sound will not travel through a vacuum. Human hearing can detect sound in the approximate frequency range 20 Hz to 20 kHz.

sound, speed of *See* **speed of sound**.

space Parts of the universe beyond Earth's atmosphere, often distinguished as interplanetary, interstellar and intergalactic space.

specific activity Number of disintegrations of a **radio-isotope** per unit time per unit mass.

specific capacitance *See* **permittivity, relative**.

specific charge Ratio of **electric charge** to unit mass of an **elementary particle**.

specific gravity Former name for **relative density**.

specific heat capacity (c) Measure of the capacity for heat of a material; the quantity of heat needed to raise the temperature of 1 kilogram of material through 1 degree. In general, if W joules of heat energy raise the temperature of a mass m from t_1 to t_2, $c = W/m(t_2 - t_1)$. Its SI units are $J\ kg^{-1}\ K^{-1}$. Alternative names: specific heat, specific thermal capacity.

specific latent heat Amount of **latent heat** per unit of mass of a substance.

specific resistance Alternative name for **resistivity**.

specific surface Surface area per unit mass or unit volume of a solid substance.

specific volume Volume of a substance per unit mass; the reciprocal of **density**.

spectra Plural of **spectrum**.

spectral line Particular **wavelength** of light in a **line spectrum**.

spectral series Sequence of lines in a **line spectrum**.

spectrometer Spectroscope that has some form of photographic or electrical detection device.

spectrometry Measurement of the intensity of **spectral lines** or **spectral series** as a function of **wavelength**.

spectrophotometer Instrument that measures the intensity of **electromagnetic radiation** absorbed or transmitted by a substance as a function of **wavelength**, usually in the visible, infrared and ultraviolet regions of the **electromagnetic spectrum**.

spectroscope Instrument for splitting various **wavelengths** of **electromagnetic radiation** into a **spectrum**, using a **prism** or **diffraction** grating.

spectroscopy Study of the properties of light, using a **spectroscope;** the production and analysis of **spectra**.

spectrum 1. Band, continuous range, or lines of **electromagnetic radiation** emitted or absorbed by a substance under certain circumstances. 2. Colored band of light or bands of colors produced by splitting various **wavelengths** of **electromagnetic radiation**, using a **prism** or **diffraction** grating.

spectrum colors Visible colors that are observed in the **spectrum** of white light (*e.g.*, in a **rainbow**).

speed Rate at which an object moves, expressed as the distance traveled in a given time; it is measured in units such as m s^{-1}, km/h or mph. Unlike **velocity**, it is independent of the direction of travel. Speed is a scalar quantity; velocity is a vector.

speed of light Velocity of light waves. Its mean value is 2.997925×10^8 m s^{-1} in a vacuum. Alternative name: velocity of light.

speed of sound Velocity of **sound** waves. In general, sound travels more rapidly through liquids than through gases, and fastest of all through solids. As temperature increases, so does the speed of sound. In dry air at 0°C, its value is 330 m s^{-1}. Alternative name: velocity of sound.

spherical aberration Type of **aberration** in a lens or mirror.

spherometer Instrument for determining the curvature of spherical objects.

spin Spinning motion (angular momentum) of an **atom, nucleus** or **subatomic particle**, assigned a quantum number of $\pm \frac{1}{2}, \pm 1, \pm 1\frac{1}{2}, \pm 2, \ldots$ Particles with whole-number spins are **bosons.**

square wave Wave motion with very rapid rise and fall times, usually describing a voltage that varies regularly and rapidly between two fixed values.

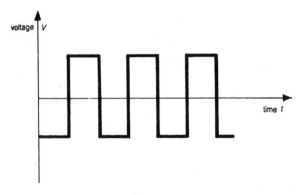

Square wave

stability Property of an object in equilibrium that opposes an attempt to move it. Any movement sets up an opposing force if an object is stable (*i.e.*, if movement raises its **center of mass**). For an object in unstable equilibrium, the slightest movement lowers the center of mass.

standard cell Electrolytic cell characterized by having a known constant **electromotive force**.

standard electrode Electrode (usually a **hydrogen electrode**) that is used as a standard for measuring **electrode potentials**. It is by convention assigned a potential of zero.

standard electrode potential Electrode potential specified by comparison with a **standard electrode**.

standard state Element in its most stable physical form at a specified **temperature** and a **pressure** of 101,325 pascals (760 mm Hg).

standard temperature and pressure (STP or s.t.p.) Set of standard conditions of **temperature** and **pressure**. By convention, the standard temperature is 273.16 K (0°C) and the standard pressure is 101,325 pascals (760 mm Hg).

standing wave Stationary wave caused by **interference** when two waves of the same wavelength move in opposite directions (*e.g.*, when a single wave is reflected back along itself).

state of matter Alternative name for **physical state of matter**.

static electricity Accumulation of **electric charge** on an object; the **electricity** produced by the removal of **electrons** from an **atom** by friction.

statics Branch of **mechanics** concerned with the study of the action of forces on stationary objects.

stationary state Characteristic energy levels of a system, as allowed by **quantum theory**.

stationary wave

stationary wave Alternative name for **standing wave**.

stator Nonmoving part of an electrical machine such as a motor or dynamo.

steam Water in the vapor or gaseous state; water above its **boiling point**. It is colorless; white "steam" contains or consists of tiny water droplets.

steam point Normal **boiling point** of water; it is taken to be a temperature of 100°C (at normal pressure).

steradian (sr) Supplementary SI unit of solid angle that is equal to the angle at the center of a sphere subtended by part of surface whose area is equal to the square of the radius.

stereophony Sound reproduction that uses two or more transmission channels, to give the hearer a similar sound to that of the original.

stereoscope Optical instrument that gives a three-dimensional illusion of depth, normally from a pair of flat photographs.

stimulated emission Process by which a **photon** causes an **electron** in an atom to drop to a lower energy level and emit another photon. It is the principle of the **laser**.

stoke C.g.s. unit of **kinematic viscosity**, equal to 10^{-4} m^2 s^{-1}. It was named after the British physicist George Stokes (1819–1903).

Stokes' law When a small sphere of radius r moves through a viscous fluid of viscosity coefficient η, the viscosity v is given by $v = 2gr^2 (d_1 - d_2) / 9\eta$, where d_1 is the density of the sphere, d_2 is the density of the medium, and g is the **acceleration of free fall**.

storage cell Alternative name for **secondary cell**.

storage device Alternative name for a computer **memory** or store. *See also* **random access memory** (RAM); **read-only memory** (ROM).

STP or **s.t.p.** Abbreviation of **standard temperature and pressure**.

strain Deformation of an object due to stress. As a quantity, it is equal to the amount of deformation divided by the original dimension. Strain has no units. *See also* **stress**.

strangeness Property of **hadrons** (subatomic particles); some of which have zero strangeness, whereas others possess non-zero strangeness because they decay slower than expected and are therefore described as strange. *See also* **spin**.

stress Any force acting upon an object in such a way as to alter its size or shape. Mechanical stress is measured in units of force per unit area. *See also* **strain**.

stroboscope Instrument consisting of a rapidly flashing lamp, employed for measuring speeds of rotation. It can also be used, by controlling the rate of flashing, to view objects that are moving rapidly with periodic motion and to see them as if they were at rest. Alternative name: rotoscope.

strontium unit (S.U.) Measure of the concentration of the radio-isotope strontium-90 in substances such as bone, milk or soil relative to their calcium content.

subatomic particle Particle that is smaller than an **atom** or forms part of an atom (*e.g.*, electron, neutron, proton). Sometimes also called an elementary particle.

subcritical Describing a **chain reaction** in a **nuclear reactor** that is not self-sustaining.

sublimate Solid formed by the process of **sublimation**.

sublimation Direct conversion of a solid substance to its vapor state on heating without melting taking place (*e.g.*, solid carbon dioxide [dry ice], iodine). The vapor condenses to give a **sublimate**. The process is used to purify various substances.

sub-shell Subdivision of an electron **shell**.

subsonic

subsonic 1. Speed less than that of the **speed of sound** in a medium. **2.** Speed that is less than Mach 1. *See* **Mach number**.

superconductivity Large increase in electrical **conductivity** exhibited by certain metals and alloys at a temperature a few degrees above **absolute zero**. Alternative name: supraconductivity.

supercooling Metastable state of a liquid in which its temperature has been brought below the normal **freezing point** without any solidification or crystallization occurring.

supercritical Describing a **chain reaction** of a **nuclear reactor** that is self sustaining.

superfluid Fluid that has practically zero **viscosity**; it forms thin films on surfaces and flows without friction (*e.g.,* liquid helium).

superheated steam Steam (under pressure) at a temperature above the boiling point of water (100°C). *See* **superheating**.

superheating Heating of a liquid or gas to above its **boiling point** in the liquid state, by increasing the pressure above that of the atmosphere. Alternative name: overheating.

superheterodyne receiver Radio receiver in which the frequency of the incoming signal is reduced by combining it with another generated in the receiver (the heterodyne principle). The resulting intermediate frequency (IF) is then amplified and demodulated.

superplasticity Property of certain materials that are able to stretch several hundred times before failing.

supersaturated solution Unstable **solution** that contains more **solute** than a **saturated solution** would contain at the same temperature. It easily changes to a saturated solution when the excess solute is made to crystallize.

supersonic Describing anything traveling through a medium faster than the speed of sound in that medium, *e.g.,* above 1,160 km/h in Earth's atmosphere at sea level. Alternative name: ultrasonic. See also **Mach number**.

surface active agent Alternative name for **surfactant**.

surface tension Force per unit length acting along the surface of a **liquid** at right angles to any line drawn in the surface. It has the effect of making a liquid behave as if it has a surface skin (which can support *e.g.*, small aquatic insects), and is responsible for **capillarity** and other phenomena. It is measured in newtons per meter (Nm^{-1})

surfactant Substance that reduces the **surface tension** of a liquid, used in detergents, wetting agents and foaming agents. Alternative name: surface active agent.

susceptibility, magnetic *See* **magnetic susceptibility**.

suspension Mixture of insoluble small solid particles and a liquid in which the insoluble substance stays evenly distributed throughout the liquid. Alternative name: suspensoid.

switch Usually mechanical device for opening and closing an electric circuit. A solid-state switch has no moving parts.

T

tachyon Theoretical subatomic particle that travels faster than light.

tape deck Unit that records audio or video signals onto, or plays back signals from, magnetic tape in cassettes or on reels.

tape punch Machine that produces punched paper tape, either operated by a **keyboard** as part of a computer **input device** or automatically as an **output device** driven by a computer.

tape reader Input device that feeds **data** off punched paper tape into a computer.

tau-particle Subatomic particle, a **lepton** and its associated anti-lepton that have unusually high mass.

telecommunications Electrical and electronic methods of communicating information (as aural or visual signals, or data) between two distant places; *e.g.*, telegraph, telephone, radio, radar, television, facsimile transmission (fax), data transmission.

telegraph Apparatus for transmitting messages over a long distance using electrical impulses sent along wires.

telemeter Device for transmitting information over long distances in modulated form, *e.g.*, by means of **radio** or **telephone**.

telemetry Technique of transmitting information by **telemeter**.

telephone Device for converting sounds into electrical impulses (which are then transmitted along wires or by **radio**) and reconverting them to sounds. It uses a **microphone** in the mouthpiece and a small **loudspeaker** in the earpiece.

telephony Transmission of **sound** by electrical means, particularly using a **telephone**.

telescope Optical instrument that forms an enlarged image of a distant object. *See also* **radio telescope; reflecting telescope; refracting telescope**.

television Method of converting visual images into electrical impulses (which are then transmitted by **radio** or along wires) and reconverting them to images.

temperature Degree of hotness or coldness of something, a measure of the average **kinetic energy** of its atoms or molecules. *See also* **temperature scale**.

temperature coefficient Change in a physical quantity with change in **temperature**, usually given as per degree rise of temperature.

temperature gradient Degree of measured rate of the **temperature** change between two points of reference in a substance or in an area.

temperature scale Method of expressing **temperature**. There are various scales, based on different **fixed points**. The **Fahrenheit scale** has largely been replaced by the **Celsius scale** (formerly centigrade), all of which express temperatures in degrees (°F and °C). In science, temperatures are frequently expressed in **kelvin** (abbreviation **K**, with no ° sign), the thermodynamic unit of temperature in **SI units**.

tempering Method of changing the physical properties of a metal or alloy by heating it for a time and then cooling it gradually or quickly.

tension Stretching force. *See also* **stress; surface tension**.

terminal In computing, an **input device** or **output device** that can handle **data**.

terminal velocity For an object falling through a fluid (gas or liquid) under the influence or gravity, the constant velocity it reaches when there is no resultant force acting on it (*i.e.,* frictional resistance equals the gravitational pull). Alternative name: terminal speed.

terrestrial magnetism Earth's **magnetism**. Alternative name: geomagnetism.

tesla SI unit of magnetic flux density, named after the Croation-born American physicist Nikola Tesla (1857–1943).

theodolite Instrument used in surveying to measure angles accurately. It is fitted with a special **telescope**.

theorem General conclusion in science or mathematics that makes certain assumptions in order to explain observations.

thermal 1. Concerning or using heat. 2. Heat-induced up-current of air, used by soaring birds and glider pilots.

thermal cross-section Probability of a **nucleus** interacting with a **neutron** of thermal energy (*i.e.,* a slow neutron).

thermal diffusion Process of forming a concentration gradient in a **fluid** mixture by the application of a **temperature gradient**. Alternative name: Soret effect.

thermal equilibrium State in which there is no net heat flow in a system.

thermalization Slowing down of fast **neutrons** to thermal energies (*i.e.,* converting them to slow neutrons, capable of initiating **nuclear fission**), achieved by a **moderator** in a **nuclear reactor**.

thermal neutron **Neutron** that has an energy of about 0.025 electrons volts (eV), and which can be captured by an atomic **nucleus** (particularly to initiate **nuclear fission**). Alternative name: slow neutron. *See also* **fast neutron**.

thermal reactor **Nuclear reactor** that has a **moderator** and in which a **chain reaction** is sustained by **thermal neutrons**.

thermal spike Transient rise in **temperature** above the normal.

thermionic emission Emission of **electrons** from a heated material (*e.g.*, the **cathode** in a **thermionic valve**).

thermionics Branch of **electronics** concerned with the study of the emission of **electrons** or **ions** from heated substances.

thermionic valve Valve (vacuum tube) with a heated **cathode** that emits **electrons**, an **anode** that collects them and often control **grids** (*e.g.*, one in a triode, two in a tetrode, etc.). Before the introduction of **semiconductor** devices, such valves were much used in electronics (*e.g.*, in amplifiers).

thermistor Temperature-sensitive **semiconductor** device whose resistance decreases with an increase in temperature, used in electronic thermometers and switches.

thermobarograph Instrument for measuring and recording the **temperature** and **pressure** of the atmosphere.

thermocouple Device for measuring **temperature** that relies on the principle that a heated junction between two dissimilar metals produces a measurable **electromotive force** (e.m.f.), which depends on the temperature of the junction.

thermodynamics Branch of **physics** concerned with the study of the effects of **energy** changes in physical systems and the relationship between various forms of energy, principally heat and mechanical energy.

thermodynamics, law of 1. First law: **energy** can be neither created nor destroyed. Alternative name: Law of conservation of energy. 2. Second law can be expressed in two ways: **entropy** of a closed system increases during a spontaneous process, or heat will not transfer spontaneously from an object to a hotter object. 3. Third law: entropy of a perfect crystal at **absolute zero** is equal to zero. 4. Zeroth law: if two objects are in thermal equilibrium with a third object, then all three are in thermal equilibrium.

thermodynamic temperature

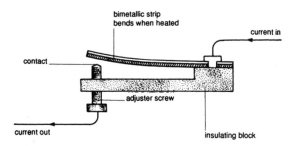

Bimetallic strip thermostat

thermodynamic temperature Alternative name for **absolute temperature**.

thermoelectricity Electricity produced from heat energy, as in a **thermocouple**.

thermograph Thermometer that records variations in **temperature** over a period of time on a graph; a self-registering thermometer.

thermometer Device for measuring **temperature**. The common liquid-in-glass thermometer relies on the expansion of the liquid (*e.g.*, mercury or dyed alcohol) in a caliberated sealed glass capillary tube.

thermometer, clinical Thermometer used in medicine for the accurate measurement of body temperature. It measures only a small range of temperatures.

thermometer, maximum and minimum Thermometer that records the maximum and minimum **temperatures** attained during a given period of time.

thermonuclear reaction Process that releases **energy** by the **fusion** of atomic nuclei (*e.g.*, of hydrogen nuclei in the **hydrogen bomb**). Alternative name: fusion reaction.

thermopile Temperature-measuring device that consists of several **thermocouples** connected in series, with one set of junctions blackened in order to absorb thermal radiation.

thermostat Device for automatically controlling the **temperature** of an appliance or apparatus. Thermostats for electrically heated appliances work by switching off the current when the required temperature is exceeded (and switching it on again when the temperature falls).

thixotropy Property of certain **fluids** that decrease in **viscosity** when placed under increased stress. "Jelly" paints are thixotropic.

Thomson effect Phenomenon in which heat is evolved when current flows along a conductor whose ends are at different temperatures; the rate of heat production is proportional to current multiplied by the **temperature gradient**. It was named after the British physicist William Thomson (1824–1907), later Lord Kelvin. Alternative name: Kelvin effect.

thyratron Gas-filled thermionic **valve** that can act as a **relay**.

thyristor Semiconductor diode, often used to control a.c. electric motors.

time base In a **cathode-ray tube**, a horizontal line on the screen produced by applying a **sawtooth wave** to the tube's deflection coils.

time sharing In computing, method of employing all or part of a system for more than one task or user, by allowing each of them in turn to have access for a fraction of a second at a time.

tonne Unit of mass equal to 1,000 kilograms. 1 tonne = 2,204.62 lb, slightly less than the imperial ton (2,240 lb). Alternative name: metric ton.

torque Turning moment produced about an axis by force acting at right angles to a radius from the axis (*see* **moment of force**).

torr Unit of pressure equivalent to that produced by a 1 mm column of mercury. It is equal to 133.3 newtons m^{-2}.

torsion Twisting force exerted on a material.

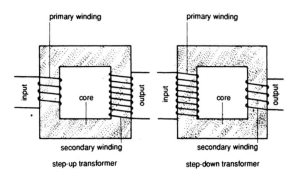

Principle of the transformer

torus Solid figure that resembles a tire or doughnut. Alternative name: anchor ring.

total internal reflection Complete reflection of a light wave at a boundary between two media (*e.g.*, glass and air). It occurs when the wave is incident at the **critical angle**.

trajectory Path followed by a moving **projectile** acted upon by gravity or other forces.

transconductance Ratio of the change in anode current to the change in grid voltage in **thermionic valve** or field-effect **transistor**.

transducer 1. Device for transforming a physical effect into a voltage, thus allowing the effect to be measured. 2. Device for converting **energy** from one form into another (*e.g.*, electrical energy to mechanical energy).

transference number Alternative name for **transport number**.

transformation, nuclear Transmutation of one atomic **nucleus** into another by means of a nuclear reaction.

transformation constant Alternative name for **disintegration constant**.

transformer Electrical device for changing the **voltage** of an **alternating current** (a.c.) without altering its **frequency**. The change in voltage (up or down) is proportional to the ratio of the turns of wire on the primary and secondary coils of the transformer; *i.e.*, if there are N_p turns on the primary coil and N_S turns on the secondary, the voltage across the secondary coil equals the voltage across the primary multiplied by N_s / N_p.

transient Momentary peak in **voltage, current** or load in an electrical circuit.

transistor Semiconductor device commonly consisting of three layers, as either *p-n-p* or *n-p-n*, where *p* and *n* refer to *n-* or *p-*type semiconductors. It allows amplification of an **electric current**, and in this application has replaced **thermionic valves**.

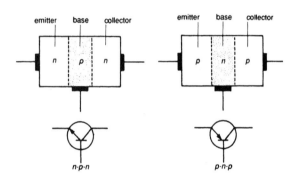

Principle of the junction transistor

transition point 1. **Temperature** at which the transformation of one form of a substance into another form can occur (usually one **crystalline** modification into another). 2. Temperature at which two solid **phases** exist at **equilibrium**. 3. Temperature at which a change to **superconductivity** happens in a substance.

transition temperature Temperature above and below which different allotropes of an element are stable.

translucent Describing a substance that transmits and diffuses light, but which does not allow a well-defined image to be seen through it. *See also* **transparent**.

transmittance Ratio of transmitted **energy** to incident energy.

transmitter 1. Apparatus that converts electrical impulses into modulated **radio waves**. 2. Mouthpiece of telephone.

transparent Describing a substance that allows light (or other **radiation**) to pass through it with little or no diffusion. *See also* **translucent**.

transport number In **electrolysis,** fraction of the total current carried by a particular **ion** in the **electrolyte**. Alternative name: transference number.

triangle of forces Triangle that denotes three **vectors,** which in turn represent three forces in **equilibrium**.

triangle of vectors Triangle whose sides represent the magnitude and direction of three **vectors** in **equilibrium** acting at a point. *See also* **parallelogram of vectors**.

triangle of velocities Triangle of vectors in which each vector denotes a **velocity**.

tritium Weakly radioactive isotope of hydrogen; it has two **neutrons** and one **proton** in its nucleus. It has a relative atomic mass of 3.016.

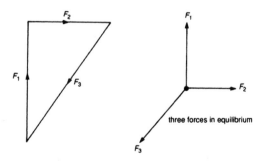

three forces in equilibrium

Triangle of three forces in equilibrium

triple point Temperature and pressure at which the three phases (solid, liquid and vapor) of a substance are in equilibrium. The triple point of water occurs at 273.16 K and 611.2 Pa. *See also* **Kelvin temperature**.

true north Geographical north, the direction toward the North Pole and the center of Earth's axis.

tuning fork Piece of metal shaped like an elongated letter U designed to produce a particular pure musical note when struck.

turbine Type of engine or motor in which jets of gas or liquid are used to drive a turbine wheel. Gas turbines (jet engines) are used extensively in aircraft, marine vessels and locomotives. Steam turbines are used to drive alternators for generating electricity.

turbulence Chaotic motion of particles in a **gas** or **liquid** when flowing through a pipe or across an aircraft wing, etc. It does not occur in laminar, or streamlined, flow.

Tyndall effect Scattering of light when a light beam passes through a colloidal solution or suspended particles of matter. It was named after the British physicist John Tyndall (1820–1893). Alternative name: Tyndall phenomenon.

U

ultra-high frequency (UHF) Band of **frequencies** in the radio spectrum between 3×10^8 and 3×10^9 **hertz**.

ultramicroscope Instrument for viewing submicroscopic objects, *e.g.*, particles of smoke and fog.

ultrasonic Describing a band of sound frequencies of about 2×10^9 hertz, which are just above the upper limit of normal human hearing. Ultrasonic energy is used in **sonar,** for degreasing (in conjunction with a suitable solvent) and for scanning soft tissues in medical diagnosis. Alternative name: supersonic.

ultraviolet radiation (UV) **Electromagnetic radiation** with wavelengths in the range 4×10^{-7} to 4×10^{-9}m, the region between visible light and X-rays. Alternative name: ultraviolet light.

uncertainty principle The limit of accuracy of the measurement of two conjugate variables of a moving object, such as its position and momentum, may be given by the relation $p_x x > h/2\pi$ where p_x is the uncertainty in the momentum, x the uncertainty in position and h Planck's constant. Alternative name: Heisenberg uncertainty principle.

uniaxial crystal Doubly refracting crystal in which there is only one direction of single refraction (*see* **double refraction**).

unified field theory Theory that attempts to describe both the electromagnetic and the gravitational theories within a single context.

unit Alternative name for kilowatt-hour, the unit that measures consumption of electricity.

unit cell Smallest group of **atoms**, **ions** or **molecules** whose three-dimensional repetition at regular intervals produces a **crystal lattice**.

universal gravitation, law of *See* **Newton's law of universal gravitation**.

unsaturated Describing a solution that can dissolve more **solute** before reaching **saturation**.

upthrust Upward force on an object immersed in a fluid, tending to make it float. *See* **Archimedes' principle**.

V

vacuum Space containing no matter. A good laboratory vacuum still contains about 10^{14} molecules of air per cubic meter (compared with about 10^{24} molecules in a liter of air at ordinary pressure); intergalactic space may have an almost perfect vacuum (although it does contain some subatomic particles).

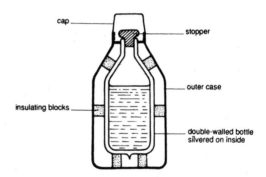

Construction of a vacuum flask

vacuum distillation Distillation under reduced pressure, which helps to lower the boiling point and hence reduce the risk of thermal dissociation. Alternative name: reduced-pressure distillation.

vacuum flask Container designed to keep hot liquids hot or cold liquids cold by minimizing heat transfer with the exterior. It consists of a stoppered double-walled glass bottle, silvered on the inside and with a vacuum between the walls, supported by blocks of insulating material in an outer protective case. Alternative name: Dewar flask, after the British chemist and physicist James Dewar (1842–1923).

vacuum pump Alternative name for **diffusion pump**.

vacuum tube Alternative name for **thermionic valve**.

valence band 1. Highest **energy level** in an **insulator** or **semiconductor** that can be filled with **electrons**. 2. Region of electronic energy level that binds **atoms** of a **crystal** together.

valence electron Electron in an outer **shell** of an **atom** that participates in bonding to other atoms to form **molecules**.

valve *See* **thermionic valve**.

Van de Graaff generator Apparatus for producing very high voltages, consisting of a large metal dome to which electrostatic charge is carried by a vertical conveyor belt. It was named after the American physicist Robert Van de Graaff (1901–1967).

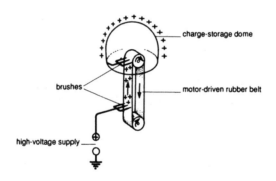

Principle of a Van de Graaff generator

van der Waals' equation (of state) Equation of state that takes into account both the volume of the gas molecules and the attractive forces between them. It may be represented as $(P + a/V^2) (V - b) = RT$, where V is the volume per mole, P the pressure, T the absolute temperature, R the **gas constant**, and a and b are constants for a given gas, evaluated by fitting the equation to experimental PVT measurements at moderate

densities. It was named after the Dutch physicist Johannes van der Waals (1837–1923).

van der Waals' force Weak attractive force induced by interaction of **dipole moments** between atoms or nonpolar molecules. It is represented by the coefficient a in **van der Waals' equation**.

Van't Hoff's law Osmotic pressure of a solution is equal to the pressure that would be exerted by the solute if it were in the gaseous phase and occupying the same volume as the solution at the same temperature. It was named after the Dutch chemist Jacobus Van't Hoff (1852–1911).

vapor A **gas** when its temperature is below the **critical temperature**; a vapor can thus be condensed to a liquid by pressure alone.

vapor density Density of a gas relative to a reference gas, such as hydrogen, equal to the mass of a volume of gas divided by the mass of an equal volume of hydrogen at the same temperature and pressure. It is also equal to half the **relative molecular mass**.

vapor pressure Pressure under which a liquid and its vapor coexist at equilibrium. Alternative name: saturation vapor pressure.

variable 1. In experimental science, property or quantity that is altered to study the resulting change in another property or quantity. Usually all others of the system are kept constant. 2. In computing, a block of data that is stored at different locations during the operation of a program.

VDU Abbreviation of visual display unit.

vector Quantity with both direction and magnitude (a quantity with magnitude only is a **scalar**).

velocity (v) Rate of movement in a particular direction; distance traveled per unit of time, measured in units such as m s^{-1}, km/h or mph. If something travels a distance d in a particular direction in a time t, its velocity is given by $v = d/t$. Velocity is a **vector** quantity, unlike **speed** (which is **scalar**, for which direction is not specified).

velocity of light *See* **speed of light**.

velocity of sound *See* **speed of sound**.

velocity ratio For a simple machine (*e.g.*, lever, pulley), the ratio of the distance moved by the load to the distance moved by the effort. Alternative name: distance ratio.

Venturi tube Cylindrical pipe with a constriction at its center. When a fluid flows through the tube, its rate of flow increases and fluid pressure drops in the constriction. The rate can be calculated from the difference in pressure between the ends of the tube and at the constriction. It was named after the Italian physicist G. Venturi (1746–1822). See also **Pilot tube**.

vernier Arrangement for measuring that permits more precise readings than a simple calibrated scale. It consists of a small movable scale graduated in intervals that are $\frac{9}{10}$ of those on the main scale, allowing the latter to be read to a tenth of a division. A circular vernier is used on a micrometer gauge. It was named after the French mathematician Pierre Vernier (1580–1637).

vertex Point at which the **optical axis** intersects the surface of **a lens**.

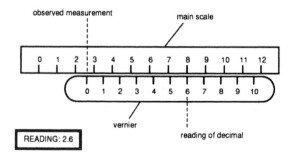

Vernier gauge

very high frequency (VHF) Describing **radio** frequencies in the range 30 to 300 MHz, used for quality radio broadcasting and line-of-sight communications.

VHF Abbreviation of **very high frequency**.

vibration Alternative name for a regular oscillation.

virgin neutron Any **neutron** from any source before collision.

virtual image Image brought to a focus by a lens, mirror or other optical system that can be seen by the eye but which cannot be focused on a screen (as opposed to a real image, which can).

viscometer Instrument for measuring **viscosity**.

viscosity Property of a fluid (liquid or gases) that makes it resist flow, resulting in different velocities of flow at different points in the fluid. Alternative name: internal friction.

visible spectrum Range of **wavelengths** of visible **electromagnetic radiation** (light), between about 780 and 380 nm.

visual display unit (VDU) Television-type screen (based on a **cathode-ray tube**) for displaying **alphanumeric** characters or graphics that represent data from a computer or word processor. Data is entered using a **keyboard, light pen** or mouse.

volatile In computing, describing stored information that is lost through a power cut.

volt (V) SI unit of **potential difference** (p.d.) or **electromotive force** (e.m.f.), which equals the p.d. between two points when one **coulomb** of electricity produces one **joule** of work in going from one point to the other.

voltage *(V)* Value of a **potential difference**, or the potential difference itself.

voltage divider Resistor that can be tapped at a point along its length to give a particular fraction of the voltage across it. Alternative name: potentiometer.

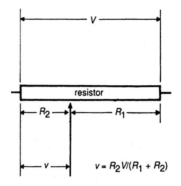

$$v = R_2 V/(R_1 + R_2)$$

Principle of a voltage divider

voltaic cell Any device that produces an electromotive force (e.m.f.) by the conversion of chemical energy to electrical energy, *e.g.*, a battery or accumulator. Alternative name: galvanic cell.

voltmeter Instrument for measuring **voltage**, or potential difference.

W

watt (W) SI unit of **power**, equal to 1 joule per second (J s^{-1}). It was named after the British engineer James Watt (1736–1819).

watt-hour Measure of electric **power** consumption. Alternative name: unit.

wattmeter Instrument for measuring electric **power** in a circuit. Power consumption is usually expressed in watt-hours, or units.

wave Regular (periodic) disturbance in a substance or in space. *E.g.*, in an airborne sound wave, alternate regions of high and low pressure travel through the air, although the air itself does not move. In an electromagnetic wave, such as light, electric and magnetic waves at right angles to each other and the direction of movement travel through a medium or through space. The distance between successive waves is the **wavelength**; the number of waves per unit time is the **frequency** of the **wave**.

wave function Mathematical equation that expresses time and space variation in **amplitude** for a wave system. *See* **Schrödinger equation**.

waveguide Rectangular- or circular-section metal tube used for carrying **microwaves** (*e.g.*, in **radar** sets).

wavelength λ Distance between successive crests, or successive troughs, of a **wave**. It is equal to v/f, where v is the **velocity** of the wave and f its **frequency**. The relationship is true for all waves, whatever their nature.

wave number Reciprocal of the **wavelength** of an **electromagnetic wave**. Alternative name: reciprocal wavelength.

wave theory of light Interference and **diffraction** phenomena of **electromagnetic waves** as explained by James Clerk Maxwell, and verified by Heinrich Hertz for **radio waves**.

weber (Wb) SI unit of magnetic flux, named after the German physicist Wilhelm Weber (1804–1891).

weight 1. On Earth, the force of gravity (9.8 m s^{-2}) acting on an object at Earth's surface; *i.e.*, weight = mass x acceleration of free fall (acceleration due to gravity). It is measured in newtons, pounds-force or dynes. *See also* **mass**. 2. Elsewhere in the universe, the force of gravity with which a star, planet or moon attracts a nearby object. Thus an object's weight is less on the moon than on Earth (although its mass remains the same).

weightlessness Property of an object that is not in a **gravitational field** or is in free fall (moving with an acceleration of g, the **acceleration of free fall**).

Wheatstone bridge Electric circuit for measuring the resistance of a **resistor** (by comparing it with three other resistors of known values). It was named after the British physicist Charles Wheatstone (1802–1875).

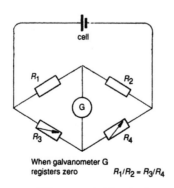

When galvanometer G registers zero $R_1/R_2 = R_3/R_4$

Wheatstone bridge circuit

Wiedemann-Franz law Ratio of electrical and thermal **conductivities** of a metal is equal to a constant times the **absolute temperature.** Alternative name: Lorentz relation.

Wilson's cloud chamber Alternative name for **cloud chamber** (after the British physicist C.T.R. Wilson, 1869–1961).

Wimshurst machine Generator of static electricity consisting of two close oppositely rotating insulating disks with pieces of metal foil on their edges. It was named after the British engineer James Wimshurst (1836–1903).

winchester 1. **Hard disk** and its drive that is small enough to use in a **microcomputer**. It was named after the city of Winchester, United States. 2. Bottle, commonly used for liquid chemicals, with a capacity of about 2.25 liters. It was named after the city of Winchester, England.

word processor Microcomputer that is programmed to help in the preparation of text, for data transmission or printing.

work (W) Energy transfer that occurs when a force f causes an object to move a distance d in the direction of the force; $W = fd$. It is measured in **joules** (newton-meters).

write head Electromagnetic device that records signals—audio, video or computer data—onto a magnetic storage medium (*e.g.,* magnetic tape or disk).

X

xerography Printing process usually employed in a photocopier. In the most common method, a projected image of the page to be copied causes loss of electric charge from a drum where the light falls on it. Resinous carbon powder (called toner) adheres to the charged areas of the drum (corresponding to the black areas of the image) and is transferred to paper and "fixed" to it with heat.

X-ray crystallography Study of **crystal** structure by examination of the **diffraction** pattern obtained when a beam of X-rays is passed through the crystal **lattice**.

X-ray diffraction Pattern of variable intensities produced by **diffraction** of **X-rays** when passed through a **diffraction grating** consisting of spacings of about 10^{-8} cm, in particular that formed by the **lattice** of a crystal.

X-ray fluorescence Less penetrating, secondary X-rays emitted by a substance when subjected to primary X-rays or high-energy electrons. The secondary X-rays are characteristic of the bombarded substance.

X-rays Electromagnetic radiation produced in a partial vacuum by the sudden arrest of high-energy bombarding electrons as they collide with the heavy atomic nuclei of a target metal. The X-rays produced are thus characteristic of the target's atoms. X-rays have very short wavelengths (10^{-3} to 1 nm) and can penetrate solids to varying degrees; this characteristic has made them useful in medicine, dentistry and X-ray crystallography. Alternative names: röntgen (roentgen) rays, X-radiation.

X-ray spectrum

X-ray spectrum Line spectrum of the intensity of **X-rays** emitted when a solid target is bombarded with electrons. It consists of sharp superimposed lines, which are characteristic of the target atoms, on a continuous background.

X-ray tube Vacuum tube designed to produce **X-rays** by using an **electrostatic field** that accelerates and directs **electrons** onto a target.

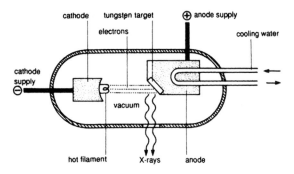

Principle of an X-ray tube

Y

yoke In electromagnetism, piece of **ferromagnetic** material that permanently connects two or more magnet cores.

Young's modulus Elastic modulus equal to longitudinal (tensile) stress divided by longitudinal strain. It was named after the British physicist Thomas Young (1773–1829).

Z

Zeeman effect Splitting of **spectral lines** of a substance into components of different **frequency** when placed in a **magnetic field**. It was named after the Dutch physicist Pieter Zeeman (1865–1943).

Zener current Current produced in an **insulator** in a strong electric field when its **valence band electrons** are raised to the **conduction band**.

Zener diode Semiconductor diode that at a certain negative voltage produces a sharp breakdown of current and hence may be used as a voltage control device. Alternative names: avalanche diode, breakdown diode.

zero energy thermonuclear apparatus (ZETA) Apparatus at the British atomic research establishment at Harwell used for studies of **fusion reactions** and **plasma** physics.

zero method Alternative name for **null method**.

zeroth law of thermodynamics *See* **thermodynamics, laws of**.

ZETA Abbreviation for **zero energy thermonuclear apparatus**.

zeta potential Potential difference that exists across the interface between a solid particle and a liquid in which it is immersed. Alternative name: electrokinetic potential.

Appendix I

SI Units

Basic Unit	Symbol	Quantity	Standard
meter	m	length	Distance light travels in vacuum in 1/299792458 of a second
kilogram	kg	mass	Mass of the international prototype kilogram, a cylinder of platinum-iridium alloy (kept at Sèvres, France)
second	s	time	Time taken for 9,192,631,770 resonance vibrations of an atom of cesium-133
kelvin	K	temperature	1/273.16 of the temperature of the triple point of water
ampere	A	electric current	Current that produces a force of 2×10^{-7} newtons per meter between two parallel conductors of infinite length and negligible cross section placed a meter apart in vaccum
mole	mol	amount of substance	Amount of substance that contains as many atoms (or molecules,

Basic Unit	Symbol	Quantity	Standard
mole (cont'd)			ions, or subatomic particles) as 12 grams of carbon-12 has atoms
candela	cd	luminous intensity	Luminous intensity of a source that emits monochromatic light of frequency 540 x 10^{12} hertz of radiant intensity 1/683 watt per steradian in a given direction

Supplementary Units

radian	rad	plane angle	Angle subtended at the center of a circle by an arc whose length is the radius of the circle
steradian	sr	solid angle	Solid angle subtended at the center of a sphere by a part of the surface whose area is equal to the square of the radius of the sphere

Derived Units

becquerel	Bq	radioactivity	Activity of a quantity of a radioisotope in which 1 nucleus decays every second (on average)

Derived Units (continued)

Basic Unit	Symbol	Quantity	Standard
coulomb	C	Electric charge	Charge that is carried by a current of 1 ampere flowing for 1 second
farad	F	electric capacitance	Capacitance that holds a charge of 1 coulomb when it is charged by a potential difference of 1 volt
gray	Gy	absorbed dose	Dosage of ionizing radiation corresponding to 1 joule of energy per kilogram
henry	H	inductance	Mutual inductance in a closed circuit in which an electromotive force of 1 volt is produced by a current that varies at 1 ampere per second
hertz	Hz	frequency	Frequency of 1 cycle per second
joule	J	energy	Work done when a force of 1 newton moves its point of application 1 meter in its direction of application
lumen	lm	luminous flux	Amount of light emitted per unit solid angle by a source of 1 candela intensity

Comprehensive Dictionary of Physics

Basic Unit	Symbol	Quantity	Standard
lux	lx	illuminance	Amount of light that illuminates 1 square meter with a flux of 1 lumen
newton	N	force	Force that gives a mass of 1 kilogram an acceleration of 1 meter per second squared
ohm	Ω	electric resistance	Resistance of a conductor across which a potential of 1 volt produces a current of 1 ampere
pascal	Pa	pressure	Pressure exerted when a force of 1 newton acts on an area of 1 square meter
siemens	S	electric conductance	Conductance of a material or circuit component that has a resistance of 1 ohm
sievert	Sv	dose equivalent	Radiation dosage equal to 1 joule of radiant energy per kilogram
tesla	T	magnetic flux density	Flux density (or magnetic induction) of 1 weber of magnetic flux per square meter

Appendix I

Basic Unit	Symbol	Quantity	Standard
volt	V	electric potential difference	Potential difference across a conductor in which a constant current of 1 ampere dissipates 1 watt of power
watt	W	power	Amount of power equal to a rate of energy transfer of (or of doing work at) 1 joule per second
weber	Wb	magnetic flux	Amount of magnetic flux that, decaying to zero in 1 second, induces an electromotive force of 1 volt in a circuit of one turn

Appendix II

Useful Formulae in Physics

Capacitance C

    $C = Q/V$, where Q = charge and V = voltage

    $C = C_1 + C_2 + C_3 + \ldots$ (for capacitors in series)

    $1/C = 1/C_1 + 1/C_2 + 1/C_3 + \ldots$ (for capacitors in parallel)

Charge Q

    $Q = It$, where I = current and t = time

    $Q = CV$, where C = capacitance and V = voltage (for a capacitor)

    $Q = F/E$, where F = force and E = electric field strength (for a stationary charge)

Current I

    $I = V/R$, where V = voltage and R = resistance

    $I = Q/t$, where Q = charge and t = time

    $I = P/V$, where P = power and V = voltage

Electric field strength E

    $E = F/Q$, where F = force and Q = charge

    $E = V/s$, where V = voltage and s = distance

Electromotive force *e.m.f.*

    $e.m.f = I/(R + r)$, where I = current and $R + r$ is the total resistance of a circuit

Power P

    $P = W/t$, where W = (electrical) energy and t = time

    $P = VI$, where V = voltage and I = current

    $P = I^2R$, where I = current and R = resistance

    $P = V^2/R$, where V = voltage and R = resistance

Resistance R

    $R = V/I$, where V = voltage and I = current

    $R = R^1 + R^2 + R^3 \ldots$ (for resistors in series)

    $1/R = 1/R^1 + 1/R^2 + 1/R^3 \ldots$ (for resistors in parallel)

Voltage V

$V = IR$, where I = current and R = resistance

$V = Q/C$, where Q = charge and C = capacitance (for a capacitor)

$V = W/Q$, where W = (electrical) energy and Q = charge

Heat

Specific latent heat L

$L = W/m$, where W = energy and m = mass

Specific thermal capacity c

$c = W/m\,(T_2 - T_1)$, where W = energy, m = mass, T_1 = initial temperature and T_2 = final temperature

Thermal capacity C

$C = W/\,(T_2 - T_1)$, where W = energy, T_1 = initial temperature and T_2 = final temperature

$C = mc$, where m = mass and c = specific thermal capacity

Mechanics

Acceleration a

$a = F/m$, where F = force and m = mass

$a = (v - u)/t$, where v = final velocity, u = initial velocity and t = time

Displacement s

$s = vt$, where v = velocity and t = time

$s = ut + \frac{1}{2}at^2$, where u = initial velocity, t = time and a = acceleration

$s = (v^2 - u^2)/2a$, where v = final velocity, u = initial velocity and a = acceleration

Distance ratio DE (= velocity ratio)

$DE = s_E/s_L$, where s_E = speed of effort and s_L = speed of load

Efficiency E

E = work obtained divided by work put in, expressed as a percentage

E = force ratio (= mechanical advantage) divided by distance ratio (= velocity ratio), expressed as a percentage

Energy W

$W = Fs$, where F = force and s = displacement

$W = mgh$, where m = mass, h = height and g = acceleration of free fall

$W = \frac{1}{2}\,mv^2$, where m = mass and v = velocity

Force F

$F = ma$, where m = mass and a = acceleratio

$F = P/v$, where P = power and v = velocity

$F = W/\,s$, where W = work (energy) and s = displacement

Force ratio FR (= mechanical advantage)

FR = load/effort

Moment of a force

moment = Fs, where F = force and s = displacement

Momentum

momentum = mv, where m = mass and v = velocity

momentum = Ft, where F = force and t = time

Power P

$P = W/t$, where W = work (energy) and t = time

$P = Fv$, where F = force and v = velocity

Pressure p

$p = F/A$, where F = force and A = area

$p = hdg$ for a liquid, where h = height (depth), d = fluid density and g = acceleration of free fall

$p = kT\,/\,V$ for an ideal gas, where k = Boltzmann constant, T = absolute temperature and V = volume

Speed S

$S = l/t$, where l = distance and t = time

Velocity v

$v = s/t$, where s = displacement and t = time

$v = u + at$, where u = initial velocity, a = acceleration and t = time

$v^2 = u^2 + 2as$, where u = initial velocity, a = acceleration and s = displacement

Work W

$W = Fs$, where F = force and s = displacement

Optics

Focal distance f

Appendix II

$1/f = 1/v + 1/u$, where v = image distance and
u = object distance
$f = r/2$, where r = radius of curvature of a mirror
$f = 1/P$, where P = power of a lens
Power (of a lens or mirror) P
$P = 1/f$
Radius of curvature r
$r = 2f$, where f = focal distance of a mirror
Reflection: angle of incidence i, angle of reflection r
$i = r$
Refraction: angle of incidence i, angle of refraction r
$\sin i/\sin r = \mu$, where μ = refractive index

Refractive index μ
$\mu = \sin i/\sin r$, where i = angle of incidence and
r = angle of refraction
$\mu = 1/\sin c$, where c = critical angle

Properties of matter
Density d
$d = m/V$, where m = mass and V = volume
Mass m
$m = F/a$, where F = force and a = acceleration
$m = W/g$, where W = weight and g = acceleration of
free fall
$m = dV$, where d = density and V = volume
Relative density RD
$RD = d_s/d_w$, where d_s = density of substance and
d_w = density of water
Weight W
$W = mg$, where m = mass and g = acceleration of free fall

Appendix III

Conversion Factors

Imperial units to metric units:

	To convert	To	Multiply by
Length	inches	millimeters	25.4
	inches	centimeters	2.54
	inches	meters	0.245
	feet	centimeters	30.48
	feet	meters	0.3048
	yards	meters	0.9144
	miles	kilometers	1.6094
Area	square inches	square centimeters	6.4516
	square feet	square meters	0.0929
	square yards	square meters	0.8316
	square miles	square kilometers	2.5898
	acres	hectares	0.4047
	acres	square kilometers	0.00405
Volume	cubic inches	cubic centimeters	16.3871
	cubic feet	cubic meters	0.0283
	cubic yards	cubic meters	0.7646
	cubic miles	cubic kilometers	4.1678
Capacity	fluid ounces	milliliters	28.5
	pints	milliliters	568.0 (473.32 for US pints)
	pints	liters	0.568 (0.4733 for US pints)
	Gallons	liters	4.55 (3.785 for US gallons)

Weight	ounces	grams	28.3495
	pounds	grams	453.592
	pounds	kilograms	0.4536
	pounds	tonnes	0.000454
	tons	tonnes	1.0161

Metric units to imperial units:

Length	millimeters	inches	0.03937
	centimeters	inches	0.3937
	centimeters	feet	0.03281
	meters	inches	39.37
	meters	feet	3.2808
	meters	yards	1.0936
	kilometers	miles	0.6214

Area	square centimeters	square inches	0.1552
	square meters	square feet	10.7636
	square meters	square yards	1.196
	square kilometers	square miles	0.3861
	square kilometers	acres	247.1
	hectares	acres	2.471

Volume	cubic centimeters	cubic inches	0.061
	cubic meters	cubic feet	35.315
	cubic meters	cubic yards	1.308
	cubic kilometers	cubic miles	0.2399

Capacity	milliliters	fluid ounces	0.0351
	milliliters	pints	0.00176 (0.002114 for US pints)
	liters	pints	1.760 (2.114 for US pints)
	liters	gallons	0.2193 (0.2643 for US gallons)

Comprehensive Dictionary of Physics

Weight			
Weight	grams	ounces	0.0352
	grams	pounds	0.0022
	kilograms	pounds	2.2046
	tonnes	pounds	2204.59
	tonnes	tons	1.1023

Appendix IV

Nobel Prizewinners in Physics

1901   W. Röntgen (German): discovery of X-rays

1902   H. Lorentz and P. Zeeman (Dutch): effect of magnetic fields on light (Zeeman effect)

1903   P. and M. Curie and H. Becquerel (French): discovery of radioactivity

1904   Lord Rayleigh (British): discovery of argon

1905   P. Lenard (German): study of cathode rays

1906   J.J. Thomson (British): gaseous discharges

1907   A. Michelson (American): measuring speed of light

1908   G. Lippmann (French): color photography

1909   G. Marconi (Italian) and K. Braun (German): wireless telegraphy

1910   J. van der Waals (Dutch): study of liquids and gases

1911   W. Wien (German): black body radiation

1912   N. Dalén (Swedish): invention of automatic gas supply for lighthouses

1913   H. Kamerlingh-Onnes (Dutch): liquefaction of gases

Comprehensive Dictionary of Physics

1914   M. von Laue (German): study of X-rays by crystal diffraction

1915   W.H. and W.L. Bragg (British): study of crystal structure using X-rays

1916   *No award*

1917   C. Barkla (British): study of light diffusion and X-ray emission

1918   M. Planck (German): quantum theory

1919   J. Stark (German): study of spectra in electric fields (Stark effect)

1920   C. Guillaume (Swiss): low-expansion nickel alloys

1921   A. Einstein (German/Swiss): photoelectric effect and mathematical physics

1922   N. Bohr (Danish): atomic structure and radiation

1923   R. Millikan (American): photoelectric effect and electronic charge

1924   K. Siegbahn (Swedish): X-ray spectroscopy

1925   J. Franck and G. Hertz (German): electron-atom interaction

1926   J. Perrin (French): atomic sizes and structure of matter

1927   A. Compton (American) and C.T.R. Wilson (British): X-ray reflection (Compton effect) and cloud chamber

1928   O. Richardson (British): thermionic emission

Appendix IV

1929 L. de Brogile (French): wave nature of electrons

1930 C. Raman (Indian): scattering of radiation by media (Raman effect)

1931 *No award*

1932 W. Heisenberg (German): quantum mechanics

1933 P. Dirac (British) and E. Schrödinger (Austrian): mathematical atomic theory

1934 *No award*

1935 J. Chadwick (British): discovery of neutron

1936 C. Anderson (American) and V. Hess (Austrian): discovery of positron and cosmic rays

1937 C. Davisson (American) and G. Thomson (British): electron diffraction by crystals

1938 E. Fermi (Italian): discovery of transuranium elements

1939 E. Lawrence (American): invention of cyclotron

1940–1942 *No award*

1943 O. Stern (German/American): study of molecular beams

1944 I. Rabi (American): study of magnetic properties of atomic nuclei

1945 W. Pauli (Austrian): exclusion principle

1946 P. Bridgman (American): high pressure physics

Comprehensive Dictionary of Physics

1947   E. Appleton (British): study of the ionosphere

1948   P.M.S. Blackett (British): study of cosmic rays

1949   H. Yukawa (Japanese): prediction of meson

1950   C. Powell (British): study of atomic nuclei and discovery of meson

1951   J. Cockcroft (British) and E. Walton (Irish): use of accelerated particles to transmute nuclei

1952   F. Bloch (Swiss-American) and E. Purcell (American): study of nuclear magnetic resonance (NMR)

1953   F. Zernike (Dutch): phase contrast microscopy

1954   M. Born and W. Bothe (German): quantum mechanics and study of electron emission

1955   W. Lamb Jr. and P. Kusch (American): study of hydrogen spectra and magnetic moment of electron

1956   J. Bardeen, W. Brattain and W. Shockley (American): invention of transistor

1957   Tsung Dao Lee and Chen Ning Yang (Chinese/American): disproof of conservation of parity

1958   P. Cerenkov, I. Frank and I. Tamm (Soviet): high-energy particles and Cerenkov effect

1959   E. Segré and O. Chamberlain (American): proving existence of antiproton

1960   D. Glaser (American): invention of bubble chamber

Appendix IV

1961 R. Hofstadter (American) and R. Mössbauer (German): study of nucleons and gamma rays

1962 L. Landau (Soviet): liquid helium research

1963 E. Wigner (American), M. Goeppert-Mayer (German/American) and J. Jensen (German): studies of structures of atomic nuclei and particles

1964 C. Townes (American), N. Basov and A. Prokhorov (Soviet): development of masers and lasers

1965 R. Feynman, J. Schwinger (American) and Sin-itiro Tomonaga (Japanese): study of quantum electrodynamics

1966 A. Kastler (French): study of atomic energy levels

1967 H. Bethe (American): theory of nuclear reactions

1968 L. Alvarez (American): study of subatomic particles

1969 M. Gell-Mann (American): classification of nuclear particles

1970 H. Alfvén (Swedish) and L. Néel (French): magnetohydrodynamics and magnetic computer memories

1971 D. Gabor (British): holography

1972 J. Bardeen, L. Cooper and J. Schrieffer (American): superconductivity

1973 I. Giaever (American), L. Esaki (Japanese) and B. Josephson (British): tunnelling effect in semiconductors

1974 A. Hewish and M. Ryle (British): discovery of pulsars and advances in radio-astronomy

Comprehensive Dictionary of Physics

1975   L. Rainwater (American), A. Bohr and B. Mottelson
(Danish): theory of atomic nuclear structure

1976   B. Richter and S. Ting (American): discovery of psi particle

1977   P. Anderson, J. Van Vleck (American) and N. Mott (British):
semiconductor development

1978   P. Kapitsa (Soviet), A. Penzias and R. Wilson (American):
low-temperature studies and discovery of cosmic
background radiation

1979   S. Glashow, S. Weinberg (American) and A. Salam
(Pakistani): unified field theory

1980   J. Cronin and V. Fitch (American): disproof of laws of
symmetry in subatomic particles

1981   N. Bloembergen, A. Schawlow (American) and K.
Siegbahn (Swedish): laser spectroscopy and high-
resolution electron microscopy

1982   K. Wilson (American): studies of changes of state

1983   S. Chandrasekhar and W. Fowler (American): evolution
and death of stars

1984   C. Rubbia (Italian) and S. van der Meer (Dutch):
discoveries of W particle and Z particle

1985   K. von Klitzing (German): electrical resistance
measurement

1986   E. Ruska, G. Binning (German) and H. Rohrer (Swiss):
electron microscope and scanning tunneling microscope

1987 J. Bednorz (German) and K. Müller (Swiss): superconductivity in ceramics

1988 L. Lederman, M. Schwartz and J. Steinberger (American): discovery of neutrinos and development of their use in research

1989 N. Ramsey, H. Dehmelt (American) and W. Paul (German): development of cesium atomic clock

1990 J. Friedman, H. Kendall (American) and R. Taylor (Canadian): discovery of structures of neutrons and protons

1991 Pierre-Gilles de Gennes (French): discovering that methods developed for studying order phenomena in simple systems can be generalized to more complex forms of matter

1992 Georges Charpak (French): invention and development of particle detectors

1993 Russell A. Hulse and Joseph H. Taylor Jr. (American): discovery of a new type of pulsar

1994 Bertram N. Brockhouse (Canadian) and Clifford G. Shull (American): pioneering contributions to the development of neutron scattering techniques for studies of condensed matter

1995 Martin L. Perl and Frederick Reines (American): pioneering experimental contributions to lepton physics

1996 David M. Lee, Douglas D. Osheroff and Robert C. Richardson (American): discovery of superfluidity in helium-3

Comprehensive Dictionary of Physics

1997 Steven Chu (American), Claude Cohen Tannoudji (French) and William D. Phillips (American): development of methods to cool and trap atoms with laser light

1998 Robert B. Laughlin (American), Horst L. Störmer (German) and Daniel C. Tsui (American): discovery of a new form of quantum fluid with fractionally charged excitations

1999 Gerardus 't Hooft and Martinus J.G. Veltman (Dutch): elucidating the quantum structure of electroweak interactions in physics

2000 Zhores I. Alferov (Russian), Jack S. Kilby (American) and Herbert Kroemer (German): basic work on information and communication technology

2001 Eric A. Cornell (American), Wolfgang Ketterle (German) and Carl E. Wieman (American): achievement of Bose-Einstein condensation in dilute gases of alkali atoms, and early fundamental studies of the properties of the condensates

2002 Raymond Davis Jr. (American) and Masatoshi Koshiba (Japanese): detection of cosmic neutrinos. And Riccardo Giacconi (American): contributions to astrophysics, which have led to the discovery of cosmic X-ray sources

2003 Alexei A. Abrikosov (Russian), Vitaly L. Ginzburg (Russian) and Anthony J. Leggett (British and American): contributions to the theory of superconductors and superfluids

2004 David J. Gross, H. David Politzer and Frank Wilczek (American): discovery of asymptotic freedom in the theory of the strong interaction

2005 Roy J. Glauber (American): contribution to the quantum theory of optical coherence. And John L. Hall (American) and Theodor W. Hänsch (German): contributions to the development of laser-based precision spectroscopy

2006   John C. Mather and George F. Smoot (American): blackbody form and anisotropy of the cosmic microwave background radiation

Appendix V

Discoveries in Physics and Its Technology

c.3000 BC Wheel (Mesopotamia)

c.450 BC Four-element theory (Empedocles)

c.400 BC Atomic theory of matter (Democritus)

c.200 BC Archimedes' principle

c.1000   Camera obscura (Arabia)

c.1100   Magnetic compass (China)

c.1100   Gunpowder rocket (China)

1260s   Spectacles (Italy)

1572   Latin translation of Alhazen's book on optics

1581   Magnetic dip discovered (R. Norman)

1590   Compound microscope (Z. Janssen)

1593   Thermometer (Galileo)

1600   Earth's magnetism described as analogous to a bar magnet (W. Gilbert)

1604   Uniform acceleration due to gravity discovered (Galileo)

1608   Telescope (H. Lippershey)

1610	Kepler's first two laws of planetary motion (third law in 1619) (J. Kepler)
1612	Clinical thermometer (Sanctorius)
1620	Submarine (C. van Drebbel)
1621	Law of refraction of light (W. Snell, published 1638)
1636	Micrometer (W. Gascoigne)
1638	Galileo publishes results of researches on motion
1642	Calculating machine (B. Pascal)
1644	Mercury barometer (E. Torricelli)
1644	Study of vacuum effects published (B. Pascal)
1650	Vacuum pump (O. von Guericke)
1654	Atmospheric pressure demonstrated (O. von Guericke)
1657	Pendulum clock (C. Huygens)
1662	Boyle's law (R. Boyle)
1665	Work on gravitation and calculus (I. Newton)
1665	Diffraction of light discovered (F. Grimaldi)
1665	Wave theory of light (R. Hooke)
1668	Reflecting telescope (I. Newton)
1669	Double refraction discovered (E. Bartholin)

Comprehensive Dictionary of Physics

1672	Reflecting telescope (N. Cassegrain)
1675	Corpuscular theory of light (I. Newton)
1676	Speed of light determined (O. Rømer)
1676	Boyle's law independently formulated (E. Mariotte)
1678	Wave theory of light (C. Huygens)
1679	Hooke's law of elasticity (R. Hooke)
1679	Pressure cooker (D. Papin)
1687	Theories of gravitation and laws of motion (I. Newton)
1687	Hygrometer (G. Amontons)
1690	Theory of light (C. Huygens)
1698	Steam engine (pump) (T. Savery)
1699	Effect of temperature on volumes of gases investigated (G. Amontons)
1702	Constant-volume gas thermometer (G. Amontons)
1704	Theories of optics (I. Newton)
1707	Atmospheric steam engine (D. Papin)
1712	Piston-operated atmospheric steam engine (T. Newcomen)
1714	Mercury thermometer (G. Fahrenheit)
1721	Reflecting telescope (J. Hadley)

1729   Aberration of light and Earth's nutation discovered (J. Bradley)

1733   Two-fluid theory of electricity (C. du Fay)

1735   Chronometer (J. Harrison)

1744   Principle of least action (P. Maupertuis)

1746   Leyden jar (P. van Musschenbroek)

1752   Lightning conductor (B. Franklin)

1757   Theory of latent heats (J. Black)

1758   Achromatic lenses (J. Dolland)

1761   Latent heat of fusion of ice (J. Black)

1764   Condensing steam engine (J. Watt)

1765   Theory of specific heats (W. Cavendish)

1768   Hydrometer (A. Baumé)

1770   Steam-powered gun carriage (N. Cugnot)

1774   Boring machine (J. Wilkinson)

1781   Law of conservation of mass (A. Lavoisier)

1783   Hair hygrometer (H. Saussure)

1783   Hot-air balloon (first manned flight by J. Pilâtre) (J.E. and J.M. Montgolfier)

1783   Manned hydrogen balloon (J. Charles)

Comprehensive Dictionary of Physics

1783   Parachute (L. Lenormand)

1783   Steamboat (paddles) (J. d'Abbans)

1785   Coulomb's law (C. de Coulomb)

1787   Charles' law (J. Charles)

1788   Blagden's law (depression of freezing point of solutions) (C. Blagden)

1788   Theories of mechanics (J. Lagrange)

1789   Combustion explained (A. Lavoisier)

1791   Effect of electric current on muscle contraction (L. Galvani)

1791   Theory of heat exchange (P. Prévost)

1794   Color blindness described (J. Dalton)

1794   Optical (semaphore) telegraph (C. Chappé)

1798   Mass (and density) of Earth determined (W. Cavendish)

1798   Study of friction-generated heat (Count Rumford)

1800   Voltaic pile (battery) (A. Volta)

1800   Electrolysis discovered (W. Nicholson)

1801   Law of partial pressures (of gases) (J. Dalton)

1801   Henry's law (on solubility of gases) (W. Henry)

1801   Ultraviolet radiation described (J. Ritter)

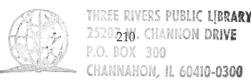

1801	Galvanic and frictional electricity shown to be the same (W. Wollaston)
1801	Submarine (R. Fulton)
1802	Gay-Lussac's law (J. Gay-Lussac)
1802	Dry battery (J. Ritter)
1803	Atomic theory (J. Dalton)
1803	Interference of light described (T. Young)
1804	Steam locomotive (R. Trevithick)
1804	Multi-wire electric telegraph (F. Salva)
1806	Beaufort's wind scale (F. Beaufort)
1808	Polarization of light described (E. Malus)
1809	Chladni's figures (of sound vibrations) (E. Chladni)
1811	Avogadro's hypothesis (A. Avogadro)
1811	Chromatic polarization discovered (D. Arago)
1813	Brewster's law (polarization of light) (D. Brewster)
1814	Fraunhofer lines in solar spectrum described (J. von Fraunhofer)
1816	Metronome (J. Mälzel)
1817	Kaleidoscope (D. Brewster)
1819	Dulong and Petit's law (P. Dulong and A. Petit)
1819	Specific heats of gases (N. Clément and C. Désormes)

Comprehensive Dictionary of Physics

1820	Electromagnetism and magnetic induction described (D. Arago)
1820	Electromagnetism described (H. Oersted)
1820	Galvanometer (J. Schweigger)
1820	Electromagnetism described (A. Ampére)
1820	Electromagnetism described (M. Faraday)
1821	Electric motor principle (M. Faraday)
1822	Seebeck (thermoelectric) effect described (T. Seebeck)
1822	Camera (J. Niepce)
1823	Mechanical calculating machine (C. Babbage)
1824	Carnot cycle (N. Carnot)
1825	Ampère's law (A. Ampère)
1825	Electromagnet (W. Sturgeon)
1825	Astatic galvanometer (L. Nobili)
1827	Ohm's law (G. Ohm)
1827	Mathematical theory of electrodynamics (A. Ampère)
1828	Electromagnet (W. Sturgeon)
1828	Nicol prism (W. Nicol)
1829	Law of gaseous diffusion (T. Graham)

1829	Practical electric motor (J. Henry)
1829	Thermopile (L. Nobili)
1830	Achromatic lenses for microscope (J. Lister)
1831	Dynamo (electromagnetic induction) (M. Faraday)
1832	Electromagnetic induction described (M. Faraday)
1832	Self-induction described (J. Henry)
1834	Peltier effect (J. Peltier)
1834	Lenz's law (H. Lenz)
1835	Coriolis effect (G. Coriolis)
1835	Electric relay (J. Henry)
1836	Moving-coil galvanometer (W. Sturgeon)
1836	Daniell cell (J. Daniell)
1836	Commutator for electric motor (W. Sturgeon)
1837	Five-wire electric telegraph (W. Cooke and C. Wheatstone)
1838	Single-wire telegraph and Morse code (S. Morse)
1840	Hess's law (of constant heat summation) (G. Hess)
1842	Doppler effect described (C. Doppler)
1842	Principle of law of conservation of energy (J. von Mayer)

Comprehensive Dictionary of Physics

1845	Faraday effect (M. Faraday)
1845	Kirchhoff's laws (G. Kirchhoff)
1845	Kinetic theory of gases (J. Waterson)
1847	Babo's law (depression of vapor pressure of solutions) (L. Babo)
1847	Law of conservation of energy developed (W. Helmholtz)
1847	Theory of electrostatic fields (Lord Kelvin)
1848	Kinetic theory of gases (J. Joule)
1848	Absolute temperature scale (Lord Kelvin)
1848	Optical activity shown to be a property of asymmetrical molecules (L. Pasteur)
1849	Speed of light determined (A. Fizeau)
1849	Mechanical equivalent of heat determined (J. Joule)
1850	Experimental proof of wave theory of light (A. Fizeau and L. Foucault)
1850	Second law of thermodynamics (R. Clausius)
1851	Rotation of Earth demonstrated (L. Foucault)
1851	Ophthalmoscope (W. Helmholtz)
1852	Law of conservation of energy formalized (Lord Kelvin)

1852	Joule-Kelvin effect (J. Joule and Lord Kelvin)
1852	Gyroscope (L. Foucault)
1852	Steerable airship (H. Giffard)
1853	Man-carrying glider (G. Cayley)
1855	Printing telegraph (D. Hughes)
1858	Refrigerator (F. Carré)
1858	Punched paper tape telegraph system (C. Wheatstone)
1859	Tyndall effect (light scattering by colloids) (J. Tyndall)
1859	First storage battery (G. Planté)
1859	Internal combustion engine (E. Lenoir)
1860	Colloids described (T. Graham)
1864	Mathematical explanation of electromagnetic waves (J. Clerk Maxwell)
1865	Entropy described (R. Clausius)
1866	Short clinical thermometer (T. Allbutt)
1866	Kundt tube (for studying sound) (A. Kundt)
1866	Leclanché dry cell (battery) (G. Leclanché)
1868	Helium discovered in solar spectrum (P. Janssen and J. Lockyer)
1868	Motorcycle (steam-powered) (E. and P. Michaux)

Comprehensive Dictionary of Physics

1869	Liquefaction of gases (T. Andrews)
1872	Vacuum flask (J. Dewar)
1872	Abbe condenser lens for microscope (E. Abbe)
1872	Study of gases at high pressures (E. Amagat)
1873	Van der Waals equation (of gases) (J. van der Waals)
1874	Crystals as (semiconductor) rectifiers (K. Braun)
1874	Multiple telegraph (A. Bell)
1876	Phase rule (J. Gibbs)
1876	Telephone (A. Bell)
1876	Internal combustion (gas) engine (N. Otto)
1877	Liquefaction of oxygen (L. Cailletet)
1877	Phonograph (T. Edison)
1878	Microphone (D. Hughes)
1879	Carbon-filament incandescent lamp (J. Swan)
1879	Electric light bulb (T. Edison)
1879	Law of heat radiation (J. Stefan)
1880	Seismograph (J. Milne)
1880	Piezoelectricity discovered (P. Curie)
1881	Hysteresis discovered (J. Ewing)

1882   Raoult's rule (on depression of freezing point of solutions) (F. Raoult)

1882   Diffraction grating (H. Rowland)

1883   Large-scale liquefaction of oxygen (Z. Wroblewski)

1884   Le Chatelier's principle (about chemical equilibria) proposed (H. le Chatelier)

1884   Multistage steam turbine (C. Parsons)

1885   Balmer series (lines in hydrogen spectrum) described (J. Balmer)

1885   Transformer (W. Stanley)

1885   Internal combustion (petrol) engine and first motorcycles and cars using it (K. Benz and G. Daimler)

1886   Germanium discovered (C. Winkler)

1886   Maxwell-Boltzmann distribution law (of gas molecular energies) (L. Boltzmann)

1886   Alternating-current motor (N. Tesla)

1887   Photoelectric effect described (H. Hertz)

1887   Movement of electromagnetic waves along wires demonstrated (O. Lodge)

1887   Existence of the ether disproved (A. Michelson and E. Morley)

1887   Gramophone (E. Berliner)

Comprehensive Dictionary of Physics

1888	Radio waves (electromagnetic waves) demonstrated (H. Hertz)
1888	Hand-held box (Kodak) camera and paper roll film (G. Eastman)
1890	Formula for frequencies of spectral lines developed (J. Rydberg)
1891	Term "electron" introduced (G. Stoney)
1891	Density of Earth determined (J. Poynting)
1892	Diesel engine (R. Diesel)
1893	Gravitational constant determined (J. Poynting)
1893	Law of hot-body radiation (W. Wien)
1894	Coherer (for detecting radio waves) (O. Lodge)
1894	Radio communications developed (G. Marconi)
1895	Curie point described (P. Curie)
1895	X-rays discovered (W. Röntgen)
1895	Photoelectric cell (J. Elster and H. Geitel)
1895	Effect of electromagnetic field on charged particles described (H. Lorentz)
1896	Radioactivity discovered (H. Becquerel)
1896	Zeeman effect (P. Zeeman)
1896	Entropy described in terms of probabilities (L. Boltzmann)

1896   Formula for distribution of black-body radiation
        (W. Wien)

1896   Experimental radio communications (A. Popov)

1896   Gyrocompass (E. Sperry)

1897   Electron discovered (J.J. Thompson)

1897   Precession of electron orbits predicted (J. Larmor)

1898   Electronic charge measured (J. Townsend)

1898   Hydrogen liquefied (J. Dewar)

1898   Submarine (J. Holland)

1898   Tape recorder (V. Poulsen)

1899   Alpha and beta rays identified (E. Rutherford)

1899   International radio communication (G. Marconi)

1900   Quantum theory proposed (M. Planck)

1900   Actinium discovered (A. Debierne)

1900   Radon discovered (E. Dorn)

1900   Gamma radiation discovered (E. Rutherford)

1901   Thermionic emission (of electrons) explained
        (O. Richardson)

1902   Kennelly-Heaviside layer proposed (O. Heaviside
        and A. Kennelly)

Comprehensive Dictionary of Physics

1902   Radio telephony (R. Fessenden)

1903   Radioactive decay series proposed (E. Rutherford and F. Soddy)

1903   Ultramicroscope (H. Siedentopf and R. Zsigmondy)

1903   Aeroplane (O. and W. Wright)

1904   Lorentz-Fitzgerald contraction (at relativistic speeds) proposed (H. Lorentz and G. Fitzgerald)

1904   Diode valve (J. Fleming)

1904   Polarization of X-rays (C. Barkla)

1905   Nuclear transmutation demonstrated (E. Rutherford and F. Soddy)

1905   Theory of special relativity (A. Einstein)

1905   Uranium decay to lead explained (B. Boltwood)

1906   Third law of thermodynamics (W. Nernst)

1906   Triode valve (L. De Forest)

1906   Lyman series (in ultraviolet region of hydrogen spectrum) described (T. Lyman)

1906   Radio broadcasting (speech and music) begins (R. Fessenden)

1908   Helium liquefied (H. Kamerlingh-Onnes)

1909   Charge on electron determined (R. Millikan)

1910   Neon lighting (G. Claude)

1911   Cloud chamber (C.T.R. Wilson)

1911   Nuclear model of the atom proposed (E. Rutherford)

1911   Superconductivity discovered (H. Kamerlingh-Onnes)

1911   Cosmic rays discovered (V. Hess)

1911   Effect of gravitational fields on light predicted (A. Einstein)

1912   X-ray diffraction demonstrated (M. von Laue)

1912   Bragg's law (of X-ray diffraction) (W. L. Bragg)

1913   Quantum theory of atoms and their spectra (N. Bohr)

1913   Isotopes discovered (F. Soddy)

1913   Geiger counter (H. Geiger)

1913   Effect of electric fields in splitting spectral lines discovered (J. Stark)

1913   Radioactive decay products quantified (K. Fajans)

1913   Atomic numbers proposed (H. Moseley)

1915   Tungsten filament lamp (I. Langmuir)

1915   X-ray spectrometer (W. Bragg)

1916   General theory of relativity (A. Einstein)

1916   Elliptical electron orbits proposed (A. Sommerfeld)

Comprehensive Dictionary of Physics

1917	Thermal diffusion of gases (S. Chapman)
1919	Mass spectrograph developed (F. Aston)
1919	Proton discovered (E. Rutherford)
1921	Nuclear isomerism explained (O. Hahn)
1922	Polarography developed (J. Heyrovsky)
1923	Scattering of radiation by electrons (A. Compton)
1923	Iconoscope television camera tube (V. Zworykin)
1924	Exclusion principle formulated (W. Pauli)
1924	Wave/particle duality of electron proposed (L. de Broglie)
1924	Presence of Heaviside-Kennelly layer demonstrated (E. Appleton)
1925	Wave mechanics introduced (E. Schrödinger)
1925	Auger effect (electron emission) discovered (P. Auger)
1925	Electron spin proposed (S. Goudsmit and G. Uhlenbeck)
1925	Television (mechanical scanning) (J. Logie Baird)
1926	First liquid-fuel rocket flight (R. Goddard)
1927	Uncertainty principle proposed (W. Heisenberg)
1927	Electron diffraction demonstrated (C. Davisson and G. Thomson)

1927   Concept of parity (in nuclear reactions) introduced
        (E. Wigner)

1928   Geiger-Müller counter (H. Geiger and W. Müller)

1928   Raman scattering effect discovered (C. Raman)

1929   Cosmic rays shown to be particles (W. Bothe)

1930   Jet engine (F. Whittle)

1930   Geodetic construction developed (B. Wallis)

1930   Cyclotron (E. Lawrence)

1930   Neutrino discovered (W. Pauli)

1930   Idea of antimatter introduced (P. Dirac)

1931   Heavy water (deuterium oxide) isolated (H. Urey)

1931   High-voltage electrostatic generator
        (R. van de Graaf)

1931   Electronic flash (for photography) (H. Edgerton)

1932   Neutron discovered (J. Chadwick)

1932   Positron discovered (P. Anderson)

1932   Artificial nuclear transformation achieved (J. Cockcroft
        and E. Walton)

1933   Muon discovered (P. Anderson)

1933   Weak interaction force (in atoms) proposed (E. Fermi)

Comprehensive Dictionary of Physics

1934   Hydrogen isotope tritium isolated (M. Harteck and P. Oliphant)

1934   Cerenkov radiation discovered (P. Cerenkov)

1934   Artificial radioactivity produced (I. and P. Joliot-Curie)

1934   Significance of slow neutrons in nuclear capture realized (H. Fermi)

1934   Two-fluid theory of superconductivity proposed (H. Casimir and C. Gorter)

1935   Meson predicted (H. Yukawa)

1935   Radar (R. Watson-Watt)

1936   Field-emission microscope (E. Mueller)

1937   Superfluidity (of helium) discovered (P. Kapitza)

1937   Muon discovered (C. Anderson)

1938   Nuclear fission discovered (by O. Hahn, as interpreted by O. Frisch and L. Meitner)

1939   Electron microscope (V. Zworykin)

1939   Betatron (D. Kerst)

1939   Single-rotor helicopter (I. Sikorsky)

1940   Plutonium discovered (G. Seaborg, *et al*)

1940   Neptunium discovered (P. Abelson and E. McMillan)

1940   Carbon-14 radio-isotope discovered (M. Kamen and S. Ruben)

1940   High-resolution electron microscope (J. Hillier)

1940   Theory of quantum electrodynamics (R. Feynman, J. Schwinger and S. Tomonaga)

1941   Jet (gas turbine) engine (F. Whittle)

1942   Nuclear fission chain reaction achieved (USA)

1942   Hydromagnetic waves in plasmas postulated (H. Alfvén)

1944   Automatic digital computer (H. Aitkin)

1944   Synchrocyclotron (V. Veksler)

1945   Atomic bomb tested (USA)

1946   Nuclear magnetic resonance (NMR) spectroscopy developed (F. Bloch and E. Purcell)

1946   Electronic computer (J. Eckert and J. Mauchly)

1947   Pion discovered (C. Powell)

1947   Radiocarbon dating (W. Libby)

1947   Point-contact transistor (J. Bardeen, W. Brattain and W. Shockley)

1947   Differences in hydrogen atom energy levels (Lamb shift) detected (W. Lamb)

1947   Supersonic flight (rocket-powered) (USA)

Comprehensive Dictionary of Physics

1948	Xerography (C. Carlson)
1948	Junction transistor (W. Shockley)
1948	Holography (D. Gabor)
1948	Long-playing gramophone record (P. Goldmark)
1949	Antiferromagnetism demonstrated (C. Shull)
1950	Unified field theory proposed (A. Einstein)
1950	Theory of nuclear structure (A. Bohr and B. Mottelson)
1951	Breeder reactor (W. Zinn)
1952	Bubble chamber (D. Glaser)
1953	Property of strangeness introduced (for subatomic particles) (M. Gell-Mann)
1954	Maser (C. Townes)
1954	Nuclear-powered submarine (USA)
1955	Antiproton discovered (O. Chamberlain, E. Segrè, C. Weigand and T. Ypsilantis)
1955	Maser (N. Basov and A. Prokhorov)
1955	Synthetic diamonds made using extremely high pressures (P. Bridgeman)
1956	Neutrino discovered (C. Cowan and F. Reines)
1956	Bound electron pairs discovered in low-temperature conductors (L. Cooper)

1957   First steerable radio telescope (at Jodrell Bank) (B. Lovell)

1957   Superconductivity explained (J. Bardeen, L. Cooper and J. Schrieffer)

1957   Mössbauer effect (R. Mössbauer)

1957   *Sputnik 1* (artificial satellite) (USSR)

1957   *Sputnik 2* (with dog) (USSR)

1958   Van Allan belts discovered (using *Explorer 1* satellite) (J. Van Allan)

1958   Tunneling effect discovered in semiconductor p-n junctions (L. Esaki)

1959   *Lunar 1* (first lunar space probes) (USSR)

1959   Hovercraft (C. Cockerell)

1960   Laser (T. Maiman)

1960   Quasars discovered (A. Sandage and T. Matthews)

1960   *TIROS 1* (first of weather satellites) (USA)

1960   *Echo 1* (radio reflector balloon satellite) (USA)

1961   Mathematical classification of fundamental particles (M. Gell-Mann and Y. Ne'eman)

1961   *Venera 1* (first Venus space probe) (USSR)

1961   *Vostok 1* (with first man in space, Y. Gagarin) (USSR)

1961   Silicon chip (USA)

Comprehensive Dictionary of Physics

1962	*Mariner 2* flies past Venus (USA)
1962	*Mars 1* launched (first probe to study Mars) (USSR)
1962	Josephson effects (B. Josephson)
1963	X-ray tomography explained mathematically (A. Cormack)
1963	*Vostok 6* (with first woman in space, V. Tereshkova) (USSR)
1964	*Ranger 7* photographs surface of moon (USA)
1965	*Mariner 4* photographs surface of Mars (USA)
1965	*Early Bird* (first active communications satellite) launched (USA)
1965	Holography (T. Gabor)
1966	*Luna 9* makes first soft landing of probe on moon (USSR)
1966	*Luna 10* becomes first probe in lunar orbit (USSR)
1966	*Surveyor 1* relays photographs from surface of moon (USA)
1968	Supersonic airliner (USSR)
1969	*Apollo 11* lands first men on moon (N. Armstrong and E. Aldrin) (USA)
1970	*Luna 16* (unmanned) returns samples of moon rock (USSR)
1971	*Mariner 9* orbits Mars (USA)

Appendix V

1971   *Salyut 1* launched (first Soviet space station) (USSR)

1971   EMI scanner (G. Hounsfield)

1973   *Skylab 1* launched (first American space station) (USA)

1974   Black holes explained (S. Hawking)

1974   *Mariner 10* flies past Venus and Mercury (USA)

1974   *Pioneer 11* flies past Jupiter (USA)

1975   *Venera 9* and *Venera 10* land on Venus (USSR)

1979   *Voyager 1* and *Voyager 2* fly by Jupiter (USA)

1979   *Pioneer 11* flies past Saturn (USA)

1981   Space Shuttle launched (USA)

1984   Sixth quark discovered (CERN)

1986   *Voyager 2* flies past Uranus (USA)

1989   *Voyager 2* flies past Neptune (USA)